LISTENING
WITH
UNDERSTANDING

LISTENING
WITH
UNDERSTANDING
DISCERNING GOD'S VOICE

CLIFFORD HILL

Sovereign World

Published by Sovereign World Ltd
PO Box 784
Ellel
Lancaster
LA1 9DA
United Kingdom

www.sovereignworld.com

ISBN: 978 1 85240 624 0

Printed in the United Kingdom

CONTENTS

CHAPTER 1

WHY LISTEN?

There is nothing more frustrating than to have an important message to communicate and nobody is listening! God Himself experienced this frustration and it is expressed many times in the Bible.

> If you would but listen to me, O Israel!
> . . .
> If my people would but listen to me,
>   if Israel would follow my ways,
> how quickly would I subdue their enemies
>   and turn my hand against their foes!
>
> (Psalm 81:8b, 13–14)

HOW NOT TO LISTEN

As a child I was not a good listener. In the classroom I was easily distracted, especially if there was a football match in progress on the sports field outside the classroom window. I can remember both my parents and my teachers exhorting me to pay more attention and to listen carefully. But it was not until I became a parent myself that I began to understand the longing in God's heart for His children to listen to Him.

My three children could hardly be more different. These differences showed up vividly in the way they listened if asked to run a simple errand. My oldest child would usually respond, "Oh, do I have to?" Following a firm response, she would question exhaustively on the detail of what she was being asked to do, probably in order to emphasise the difficulties and the burden being placed upon her. My second child, in total contrast, was all eagerness. In fact she was so keen to get going that she rarely stopped to hear what she was being asked to do and she would therefore fly off only half-prepared.

My third child was completely laid-back. He lived in a little world of his own from which he only occasionally emerged to join the rest of the family. He would stand there giving all the appearance of rapt attention but I knew from experience that he was not listening to a word I was saying. I would have to say it time and again: "Now listen carefully . . ." But even so, he was quite capable of setting off on an errand and coming back some time later having forgotten where he was supposed to go.

I should add that all my three children have now outgrown their childish ways and become beautiful believers in the Lord Jesus. The character defects they inherited from their parents have been transformed by the grace of God. I am grateful to them for enabling me to perceive things from the perspective of a father rather than that of a child.

The three different responses of my children to a request to run an errand represent three of the different ways we listen to God:

- dutifully but lacking enthusiasm
- eagerly but carelessly and without discernment
- inattentively and lacking in concentration

None of these is good and it is the purpose of this mini-book to examine the right response to the Father's plea that we should listen to Him.

Since writing this chapter those nearest and dearest to me have reminded me that I have not entirely outgrown my childhood weaknesses as well as my children have. I too tend to live in a little world of my own in which I do not always hear what is going on around me. I have been known to telephone my personal assistant and say, "Jean, I'm at Euston station – where am I going?" And she would respond, "Well, you should be at King's Cross because you're going to York!"

I defend myself by saying I have more important things on my mind than the humdrum details of train times and destinations. But the real point of making this confession of my inattentiveness in listening to travel instructions faithfully given me by my PA, and even messages given to me by my wife, is to say that if I can train myself, as I have done over many years, to listen carefully to God, then this should be an encouragement to others who, like me, are poor listeners.

THE FATHER'S DESIRE

It is the Father's deepest desire that His children should listen to Him. Throughout the history of Israel God used the prophets to plead with His people to listen to Him:

> Listen to me, O Jacob,
>> Israel, whom I have called:

I am he;
  I am the first and I am the last.
My own hand laid the foundations of the earth,
  and my right hand spread out the heavens;
when I summon them,
  they all stand up together.

Come together, all of you, and listen . . .

Come near me and listen to this . . .

This is what the LORD says . . .
"I am the LORD your God,
  who teaches you what is best for you,
  who directs you in the way you should go.
If only you had paid attention to my commands,
  your peace would have been like a river,
  your righteousness like the waves of the sea."

(Isaiah 48:12–18; my emphasis)

This passage shows us why we should listen carefully to the Father, because the Lord our God knows what is best for us and He is the only one who can direct our steps into the paths of peace and righteousness. Just as a human father knows the dangers that face an unsuspecting child and is therefore able to warn his children, so God knows the things we are facing and longs to warn us of the approach of danger. On the positive side, God also longs to teach us what is right. Just as human parents instruct their children to distinguish between right and wrong, so the Lord watches over us and teaches us the ways of righteousness because He knows that these are for our good and lead to joy and happiness and a true sense of fulfilment; by contrast, when we follow the paths of evil, they lead to disaster and end in misery until, like the prodigal son, we come to our senses and seek to return to the Father.

Part of growing up is to recognise that our parents really do have more experience of the pitfalls of life and therefore more wisdom and understanding than we have as children. Mark Twain humorously remarked that when he was a teenager he was surprised to discover how ignorant his father was, but when he reached more mature years as an adult he was amazed to discover how much his father had picked up in the meantime! If our parents are wise and trustworthy we have confidence in following their teaching, even if it conflicts with our own desires and selfish ambition. There are lessons to be learned from this in regard to our personal relationship with God. As we grow in spiritual maturity our understanding of the fatherhood of God increases and so too does our trust. As we move from a second-hand knowledge based upon the teaching of others to a personal encounter with God through the Lord Jesus Christ, so our confidence becomes rooted in the absolute trustworthiness of God our Father.

THE FATHER'S GOOD PLANS

In the spiritual life, as we grow in maturity, we are able to recognise the hand of God in guiding our lives. We recognise that He has good plans for us. Jeremiah reassured the exiles in Babylon that God had not forgotten them:

> "For I know the plans I have for you," declares the LORD, "plans to prosper you and not to harm you, plans to give you hope and a future."
>
> (Jeremiah 29:11)

He went on to reassure them that although they were in enemy territory and suffering under oppression, God was still watching over them and would hear their cries if they would only call out to Him:

> Then you will call upon me and come and pray to me, and I will listen to you.
>
> (Jeremiah 29:12)

But Jeremiah knew it was not just a matter of crying out to the Lord in distress as a last hope; it was essential that the people should be wholehearted in seeking God. His promise was,

> "You will seek me and find me when you seek me with all your heart. I will be found by you," declares the LORD . . .
>
> (Jeremiah 29:13–14)

God is not reluctant to communicate with us, His children. Throughout the Bible He is shown as a God who communicates with His people. From the time He spoke to Adam in the Garden to the time when he spoke to John on the island of Patmos, giving him the messages to the seven churches and the revelation of the last days, God continually spoke to His people, to all those whose ears were open to hear Him. He did so, not in anger, but in love. It was because of His great compassion for His children that He spoke to them:

> As a father has compassion on his children,
>   so the LORD has compassion on those who fear him;
> for he knows how we are formed . . .
> from everlasting to everlasting

the LORD's love is with those who fear him,
 and his righteousness with their children's children –
with those who keep his covenant
 and remember to obey his precepts.

(Psalm 103:13–18)

THE FATHER'S GREAT LOVE

Those of His children who respond to His love discover that God is truly like a Father whose love for His children is unending and unbreakable. He is one who keeps His covenant; He will never break His promise. He is utterly trustworthy and dependable. He will keep His word. Time after time the prophets had to teach the people that it was because of their own disobedience and failure to listen to the Lord that things went wrong in the life of the nation as well as in their own individual lives. Isaiah declared,

Yet the LORD longs to be gracious to you;
 he rises to show you compassion.
For the LORD is a God of justice.
 Blessed are all who wait for him!

(Isaiah 30:18)

Isaiah went on to say that even when, through our own sinfulness, everything goes wrong and we eat "the bread of adversity" (30:20), if we will only turn humbly in repentance to our God He will listen and He will actually speak to us, showing us the right path.

Whether you turn to the right or to the left, your ears will hear a voice behind you, saying, "This is the way; walk in it."

(Isaiah 30:21)

Jeremiah had the saddest and most demanding ministry of all the prophets. For forty years he warned the leaders and the people of Jerusalem and Judah that God would not protect an unholy, disobedient people who deliberately flouted His laws, failed to put their trust in Him, ignored the warning signs He sent to them and actually worshipped other gods, turning away from the one true God and exalting idols. Time after time Jeremiah had to declare the same message about listening to God. This was what the Lord said:

> I spoke to you again and again, but you did not listen; I called you, but you did not answer . . .
>
> For when I brought your forefathers out of Egypt and spoke to them, I did not just give them commands about burnt offerings and sacrifices, but I gave them this command: Obey me, and I will be your God and you will be my people. Walk in all the ways I command you, that it may go well with you. But they did not listen or pay attention; instead, they followed the stubborn inclinations of their evil hearts . . . day after day, again and again I sent you my servants the prophets. But they did not listen to me or pay attention.
>
> (Jeremiah 7:13b, 22–26)

The Bible shows that God spoke to His people clearly so that they would know Him and be able to understand His nature and His purposes. He wanted them to know how much He loved them so that they would respond to His love by loving and trusting Him. It was for this reason that He revealed Himself to the patriarchs and spoke clearly to His servant Moses and to the early non-writing prophets such as Nathan, Elijah and Elisha and later to the great writing prophets from Amos to Malachi. For those who were prepared to listen to the Lord He gave guidance and encouragement as well as warnings and rebuke.

Joshua provides us with a good illustration of the necessity for listening carefully to the Lord and doing only what He tells us to do. Joshua was well aware of the dangers confronting him when he crossed the River Jordan and began to move into Canaan. His advance party had given him information concerning the defences and the strength of the opposition facing him in Jericho. Joshua received from the Lord clear instructions outlining the strategy for taking Jericho. The strategy, from a human standpoint, appeared crazy. But Joshua trusted the Lord; he carried out the instructions faithfully and the victory followed – a victory in which all the glory was given to God.

Flushed with success, Joshua headed for his next objective, the city of Ai. Once again he sent a reconnaissance party who not only reported on the city's defences but recommended a battle plan. Without consulting the Lord, Joshua accepted this plan and gave orders for a small number of men, as suggested by the advance party, to go and take Ai. The result was death and humiliation, which could have led to disaster for all the people if the Canaanites had been swift to gather from the whole region and drive the Israelites out before they were established in the land.

Joshua fell on his face and wept before God all day. Eventually God spoke to him, telling him to get up and face the situation. This time Joshua listened to the Lord, and victory followed. God is not a hard taskmaster. On the contrary, He is a loving Father, always ready to forgive us even when we have gone disastrously wrong. He longs for us to be in a right relationship with Himself and He has provided the way through Jesus, His precious Son.

Choosing to listen

We can choose what we listen to. A friend of mine who is a dairy farmer and also has several children told me his wife sometimes says in the morning that she has had a bad night with the baby and had to get up five times. He says in reply, "Well, I had a great night – I didn't hear a thing!" But if one of his cows is calving he hears the first sound she makes out in the yard. He says, "I'm out of bed, dressed and out in the barn in a few minutes. I stay with her until she is through her labour, safely delivered, and both she and the calf are comfortable; then I go back to bed. In the morning I tell my wife about the new calf and that I've been up for most of the night and she says, 'Well, I had a great night – I didn't hear a thing!'"

We can all choose what we hear. We can train ourselves to shut out what we don't want to hear and to tune in to what we regard as important. We can do this in our spiritual life just as well as in physical things. Most Christians are far too preoccupied with the things of the world to listen to God. We spend many hours each day listening to TV or radio or tapes or listening to other people, but we spend very little time alone seeking the presence of the Father. But before we can choose to listen, we have to want to listen.

Wanting to listen

If I have learned anything from my own experience it is that we have to *want* to listen. Although as a child I had to be coaxed (or driven!) to learn some subjects like mathematics in which I was not the least bit interested, by the time I reached university I was an eager student with a thirst for knowledge that drove me to do four degrees. I have discovered that I only listen attentively to what I *want* to hear and I "switch off" from the rest. Hence I taught myself New Testament Greek in a barrack room while doing National Service, oblivious to the noise around me. I realised some years ago that in order to fulfil the ministry to which God was calling me I had to want to listen to Him more than anything else in life. It had to be my chief desire to hear from Him and to hear rightly. In order to achieve this I had to exercise my will to listen and to shut out the distractions around me.

If we truly seek Him with all our heart we will certainly come to know Him, for the Father has not only sent the Son to cleanse us from sin, but He has also poured out His Holy Spirit upon all believers. Through the ministry of the Holy Spirit we can communicate with the Father. But first we have to learn to listen like little children listening to their parents whom they love and trust because they know themselves to be loved. Learning to listen is one of the most exciting parts of our walk with God. God's solemn promise is known to many Christians through the familiar words of Mendelssohn's *Elijah*: "If with all your heart ye truly seek me, ye shall ever surely find me." These words are based upon the promise given through the prophet Jeremiah to the exiles in Babylon whom he was seeking to comfort during their forcible exile from Jerusalem:

> You will seek me and find me when you seek me with all your heart.
>
> (Jeremiah 29:13)

QUESTIONS

1. What are the qualities of a good listener and how would you rate yourself and others in your group?
2. Why does God want to communicate with us?
3. Why should we learn to listen to God?
4. Jeremiah 29:1–14. God has good plans for His people Israel. Is this still true today? And does it also apply to the Church?

CHAPTER 2

LISTENING WITH UNDERSTANDING

L istening does not come naturally, although some people are naturally more receptive than others. It depends largely upon how fully we are dominated by the drive towards self-fulfilment. There are some people who are so taken up with their own concerns that they never really hear what other people are saying, even when they are being spoken to directly. We are all of us, to a certain degree, selective in what we hear. We are able to tune out those things that appear irrelevant, or threatening, or even simply unpleasant – things that we do not wish to face.

If we are to benefit from the things that we hear, that is, to add to our store of knowledge and grow in wisdom, we have to learn to interpret the things we hear and see around us. But it is not enough simply to listen; we have to learn to listen with *understanding*. In the natural realm, this process begins at birth, and even before that. The unborn child hears his mother's voice and the sounds that surround her. As soon as the young child is able to focus his eyes, he begins to associate those sounds and pictures first heard in the womb, and the lifelong process of learning to interpret them begins.

LEARNING TO INTERPRET

A similar process takes place in the spiritual life. Because we are created in the image of God, even before we are born again, we begin to hear sounds that we are vaguely aware are associated with God. This is the significance of Jeremiah's conviction that his call to ministry was given by God even while he was still in the womb. His testimony is,

> The word of the LORD came to me, saying,
>
> "Before I formed you in the womb I knew you,
> before you were born I set you apart;
> I appointed you as a prophet to the nations."
>
> (Jeremiah 1:4–5)

Many believers, especially those called into the preaching and pastoral ministry, could give a similar testimony. It is, nevertheless, only after our spiritual rebirth that we can come to appreciate the significance of the spiritual events in our lives. With increasing spiritual maturity our "inner eyes" and "ears" are opened so that our understanding of the significance of things that are being communicated to us grows. Just as a very young child can understand when his mother or father is pleased or displeased with him by the tone of voice or by the look on their faces and their body language, so we learn to interpret the spiritual sounds and signs of the Father's communication to us.

The prophets had none of the advantages that we have of drawing upon the revelation brought to us through Jesus our

Messiah. They had to learn to listen to God and they also had to learn to listen with understanding. This was one of the qualities that distinguished them from other people. The prophets, however, were not the only ones who heard from God. There are plenty of accounts in Scripture of God speaking to men and women from the time of Adam and Eve. He spoke to the patriarchs, to the judges, to the leaders of Israel and to the apostles in New Testament times.

Throughout the early days in the history of Israel, especially in the period of the judges and into the time of the monarchy, there were many to whom God spoke personally. It was only during the time of the monarchy that political and religious leadership became separated in Israel. In earlier times, those who exercised leadership in the nation were men or women of deep commitment to God who learned to listen to Him and to draw strength and encouragement as well as guidance in the exercise of leadership.

Leaders such as Moses, Joshua, Gideon, Deborah and even King David learned to listen to the Lord before taking initiatives in leadership which would commit the nation to any particular course of action. They realised that the destiny of the nation was in their hands. The decisions they made would affect not only their own life but that of the whole nation, which was an enormous burden of responsibility. This is reflected in one of the many conversations that Moses had with God before he and the Israelites embarked on the journey that would take forty years before reaching their destination in the promised land of Canaan. Moses pleaded with God on behalf of the nation. He said,

> If you are pleased with me, teach me your ways so I may know you and continue to find favour with you. Remember that this nation is your people.
>
> (Exodus 33:13)

God's response to this was,

> My Presence will go with you, and I will give you rest.
>
> (Exodus 33:14)

This was exactly the assurance that Moses needed, but because of the enormity of the task to which he was being called, he continued to seek further assurance, saying,

> If your Presence does not go with us, do not send us up from here. How will anyone know that you are pleased with me and with your people unless you go with us? What else will distinguish me and your people from all the other people on the face of the earth?
>
> (Exodus 33:15–16)

This two-way conversation between Moses and God is a beautiful illustration of the intimacy of the relationship that Moses enjoyed with God. Of course Moses was unique in that God had been preparing him throughout his life for this formative moment in the history of the nation, but God is an unchanging God in His nature and purposes, and He offers today the same level of intimate relationship to those whose lives are committed to Him, to seek Him, to know Him and to serve Him.

The leaders of Israel whose own spiritual lives were constantly refreshed by this communication with God provide a model for us today. Their personal relationship with God was often reflected in the level of faith they were able to communicate to those who looked to them for leadership. It was no doubt because the 300 men in Gideon's tiny army believed that he had received the strategy for battle directly from God that they were prepared to surround the Midianite camp armed only with a torch, an earthenware jar and a trumpet! Similarly, the men who marched seven times around the city of Jericho under Joshua's command must have had a powerful conviction that God had spoken to their leader before undertaking what surely appeared to be a highly improbable and impracticable strategy.

The kingship of David came to be idealised in Israel because of his personal relationship with God which gave us so many beautiful psalms such as Psalm 23, "The Lord is my Shepherd". David had learned to listen to God whilst still a young boy when he was tending his father's flock on the Judean hills around Bethlehem. Many of the later kings of Israel and Judah lacked this personal relationship with God, never learning to hear from Him themselves and often deeply resenting the Word of the Lord brought to them by the prophets. It was during their reigns that God raised up prophets, men or women who were hearing from Him, who had not only learned to listen and to interpret but who also had the courage to declare publicly what they were receiving. It was, of course, the anointing of the Spirit of God upon their lives that distinguished the prophets from other people. When God spoke to them He not only gave them the Word but also the power and authority to declare it. He even opened the way ahead of them to declare it to kings and rulers so that the Word of God was delivered directly to those who ought to be hearing from God.

It is arguable that if the leaders, throughout the history of Israel, had been men of God, listening to Him with understanding, there would have been no need for the separate office of the prophet. Certainly it was the wish of Moses that the Spirit of God should come upon all the people, which would enable them to prophesy – that is, to declare the Word of God publicly. This is powerfully expressed in the account in Numbers 11 of Moses encountering great problems of leadership in the early days after the Israelites' deliverance from Egypt. He was having particular problems feeding the nation in a hostile environment, so he talked to the Lord, asking,

> Where can I get meat for all these people? They keep wailing to me, "Give us meat to eat!" I cannot carry all these people by myself; the burden is too heavy for me.
>
> (Numbers 11:13–14)

In his desperation Moses even went so far as to cry out,

> If this is how you are going to treat me, put me to death right now . . .
>
> (Numbers 11:15)

God's response was to call for the seventy elders of Israel to come before Him in the Tent of Meeting. His promise was,

> I will come down and speak with you there, and I will take of the Spirit that is on you and put the Spirit on them. They will help you carry the burden of the people so that you will not have to carry it alone.
>
> (Numbers 11:17)

It is reported that when the Spirit of God rested upon these men they prophesied, although it is not clear from the text whether this was a one-off experience or whether they continued to exercise this ministry. What is clear, however, is that two of the elders were missing from the meeting, yet the Spirit of God came upon them while they were still in the camp. This was reported to Moses, who responded,

Are you jealous for my sake? I wish that all the LORD's people were prophets and that the Lord would put his Spirit on them!

(Numbers 11:29)

In hindsight, we are able to see how Moses' wish was fulfilled at Pentecost when the Spirit of God was indeed poured out upon all believers who had come into a right relationship with the Father through faith in the Lord Jesus.

ALL BELIEVERS CAN LISTEN

The Holy Spirit, which was given to the Church at Pentecost, has never been withdrawn. Through Him all believers are able to hear from God and to listen with understanding. It is for this reason that Paul urges the Corinthians eagerly to desire spiritual gifts, "especially the gift of prophecy" (1 Corinthians 14:1).

This does not mean that Paul envisages all believers exercising the *ministry* of the prophet. Paul expects all believers to learn to listen to God and to listen with understanding so that He may speak into our individual lives and may speak through all believers into the lives of their families and their immediate circle of friends, including the local church. This also means that the whole body of believers worldwide will be able to discern the significance of contemporary events and understand the way God is working out His purposes in the present time; they will be able to declare the Word of God to unbelievers, thus fulfilling the Great Commission and hastening the day when people from all nations will have heard the gospel and had the opportunity of receiving Jesus as their personal Lord and Saviour.

It is in this way that the whole Church becomes "a prophetic people", and the whole Body of Christ worldwide becomes armed with the spiritual weapons of warfare appropriate to the days in which we live and able to declare the Word of the Living God with power and authority. These have always been the prophetic marks to be seen upon the lives of the servants of God.

There are still some individuals who are called specifically to the ministry of the prophet, which is to the wider Church as God opens the doors and gives the opportunity. This is in the same way as He did for men like Agabus, Judas and Silas, who exercised prophetic ministries among the churches of Judea and Asia Minor in New Testament times. But their ministries should not be confused with the "gift of prophecy" which all believers can exercise within their own sphere of influence.

DISCERNING GOD'S VOICE

God wants His people to be a listening people, and just as the prophets in Scripture had to learn to listen with understanding so we have to learn to listen today. The first part of learning to listen to God is to recognise His voice. If we don't know who is speaking we shall be in confusion from the very start. It is for this reason that John urged all the believers in the early Church,

> Do not believe every spirit, but test the spirits to see whether they are from God . . .
>
> (1 John 4:1)

It is extremely important that we learn to discern the source of the message we are hearing. This is particularly relevant today because we live in a day of deception when there are many false prophets, false "christs", and false teachers whose teaching is confusing and misleading many people. Just as a young baby has to learn to distinguish the voice of his own mother and father, so we have to learn to recognise the voice of our Heavenly Father. This recognition does not come naturally, although God has made provision for it by giving us His Spirit. The prophets had to learn to recognise the voice of God before they could begin to learn understanding or go on to the more demanding and complex part of their ministry: that of interpreting signs, pictures and visions.

The boy Samuel did not recognise God's voice when He first spoke to him. He heard his name spoken and thought Eli must have called because at this time "Samuel did not yet know the LORD: The word of the LORD had not yet been revealed to him" (1 Samuel 3:7). God could not reveal His Word to him until Samuel was thoroughly familiar with the sound of God's voice. The first step was his willingness to listen, signified by his response:

> Speak, LORD, for your servant is listening.
>
> (1 Samuel 3:9)

From childhood, Samuel had had a willing and teachable spirit. He had been willing to do the humblest tasks of service, assisting the priest in carrying out his religious duties. A willing heart and a teachable spirit are essentials if we are to have the right attitude of humility, reverence and obedience in seeking to listen to the Lord.

The Lord our God is a consuming fire (Hebrews 12:29) who will not reveal Himself to those who are arrogant, haughty or puffed up with pride or trusting in their own wisdom. Our attitude has to be right in our approach to God. It is for this reason that Jesus says we have to become like little children who have a simple trust in their father and who know that they have no great ability themselves. Grown men and women who have acquired much learning or who have exercised great responsibility in their daily lives find it the most difficult to approach God with childlike simplicity. Their needs are beautifully expressed in Psalm 51 where the psalmist praises God for teaching him "wisdom in the inmost place" (verse 6) and concludes:

> The sacrifices of God are a broken spirit;
>   a broken and contrite heart,
>   O God, you will not despise.

(Psalm 51:17)

It is this experience of brokenness – that is, broken from our human desires, ambitions, pride and trust in our own abilities – that provides the key to understanding how we enter into the presence of God. Jeremiah calls this "standing in the council of the Lord". In referring to the false prophets he asks the question,

> But which of them has stood in the council of the LORD
>   to see or to hear his word?
> Who has listened and heard his word?

(Jeremiah 23:18)

Every preacher needs to face the fact that if he has not learned to enter the "council of God" he cannot declare the Word of God; he can only offer his own human opinions. The tragedy is that from a large number of church pulpits it is only trite little human homilies that are offered; the majestic Word of God through which the preacher is able to declare, "Thus says the Lord!" is only rarely heard. But it is not only preachers who need to take note of this warning. Every believer, according to Paul's teaching, is able to declare the Word of God. But we cannot do this unless we have learned to listen and to heed the Word of the Lord. If we are known to be believers and others come to us for counsel, the words we offer will not be from the Lord unless we have learned to listen to Him and to recognise His voice.

The prophets also had the more complex task of learning to interpret "signs", that is, events that occurred during their lifetime, or things that they saw with their physical eyes that had some spiritual significance. There are numerous examples in the Prophets such as the catalogue of catastrophes that occurred in northern Israel during the ministry of Amos, to which he referred when preaching at Bethel. Everyone knew of the events of which he spoke: the drought, the bad harvest, crop disease, the plague of locusts and other hardships which had brought suffering to the people. Amos concluded each reference with the words,

"Yet you have not returned to me," declares the LORD.

(Amos 4:6–12)

Jeremiah also used similar incidents in this way. He was constantly watching contemporary events and seeking the Lord for their spiritual significance. But it was because Jeremiah had learned to enter the presence of the Living God that he was able to give the meaning of these events or the reason why they had occurred and to make his pronouncements with such authority:

You have defiled the land
    with your prostitution and wickedness.
Therefore the showers have been withheld,
    and no spring rains have fallen.

(Jeremiah 3:2b–3a)

INTERPRETING THE SIGNS

God can speak through anything, including ordinary everyday

events. The prophets also had to learn to interpret visions and pictures which they received because God sometimes reveals His Word to us in a pictorial manner. At the beginning of Jeremiah's ministry God spoke to him, asking, "What do you see, Jeremiah?" and he replied, "I see the branch of an almond tree" (Jeremiah 1:11). He was then given the interpretation of this and again the Lord asked, "What do you see?"; this time he answered, "I see a boiling pot, tilting away from the north" (Jeremiah 1:13). Once again he was given the interpretation, followed by directions for carrying out his ministry and delivering the Word that God would reveal to him during the next forty years of his life.

Ezekiel's prophetic ministry began in an even more dramatic manner, with a vision of a great windstorm that climaxed with him seeing the figure of a man surrounded by a rainbow in the clouds.

> This was the appearance of the likeness of the glory of the LORD. When I saw it, I fell face down, and I heard the voice of one speaking.
>
> (Ezekiel 1:28b)

This seemed to set the pattern for Ezekiel's ministry as we have more visions recorded by him than by any other prophet. But visions have to be interpreted, and it is notable that Ezekiel never simply had the experience of the vision without the accompanying voice of the Lord speaking to him and giving him a spiritual understanding of what he was seeing. He too, like the boy Samuel and all the other prophets, had to learn to listen and to recognise the voice of the Living God.

Listening with understanding is the first prerequisite of being able to declare the Word of God, or to give wise counsel or even to be able to receive a word from the Lord into our own personal lives. God wants all His people to be able to listen with understanding.

LISTENING IN THE QUIET TIME

If you want to hear from God you have to set aside time. It is no good being in a hurry and simply rushing into the presence of God with all the pressures of the world dominating your mind. You will be disappointed. If it really is important to us to listen to the Lord, we have to find time in our lives, however busy we are. Henry Thornton, close friend of William Wilberforce and author of the first book of family prayers to be published in Britain, was once asked what was the ideal amount of time to be spent in prayer each day. Thornton replied, "About two hours, I should say. Unless, of course, you are very busy. In that case it should be more!"

The best time of the day to set aside time for prayer is, of course, a matter of personal choice. There is much to be said for using the early mornings. In my student days I found it very difficult to wake up in the mornings. I could stay up very late at night discussing complex theological arguments or ethical dilemmas (setting the world right!) but mornings were a problem. Even the use of an alarm clock, plus the aid of my friends (often unwelcome!), only produced a kind of robotic activity. I would go through the motions of being alive until mid-morning, by which time I was fully awake; this would be about halfway through the first lecture of the day. Once I was ordained I had to exercise personal discipline in the use of my time and I slowly taught myself to wake early at a regular hour. I discovered that the early hours of the day, before the telephone rings, the postman comes, or the e-mails start pouring in, provide the best opportunity for a quiet time of prayer.

Actually, it's not quite true to say that "I discovered it" because I learned it from Isaiah. He describes how he learned to wake early in the morning and shake off the spirit of weariness. He learned to be quiet and to listen to the Lord. He says,

> The Sovereign LORD has given me an instructed tongue,
>> to know the word that sustains the weary.
> He wakens me morning by morning,
>> wakens my ear to listen like one being taught.
>
> (Isaiah 50:4)

His description of listening attentively, like a student sitting at the feet of his favourite professor, made a lasting impression upon me. Waking early became natural, and many times I've had the experience of God actually waking me and speaking to me or reminding me of something that He had dropped into my mind during the night. For many years I've made a habit of waking early and using those first precious moments, before having any human conversation, of simply allowing the presence of God to surround me and His glory to fill my spirit so that He can alert me to anything of which I ought to be aware for the coming day. It is particularly useful, if you are facing a difficult situation, to put on the whole armour of God before facing the demands of the day.

The early hours of each day should not be squandered in unnecessary sleep, but used particularly for recalling anything that God may have said during the night; as Paul did when he received the vision of the man of Macedonia (Acts 16:9) which changed the course of his life and redirected his missionary itinerary. God loves to communicate with His children, which He does in many different ways. We can so easily miss what He is saying to us if we are not attentive. Learning to use a regular time is by far the most beneficial way.

QUESTIONS

1. 1 Corinthians 1:18 – 2:5. Is human wisdom a help or hindrance in understanding what God is saying to His Church today?

2. Matthew 28:19–20. How does listening with understanding help the Church to fulfil the Great Commission?

3. 1 John 4 teaches that prophetic revelation can come from different sources. How do we discern the source of what we are hearing?

4. Ezekiel 37 is a classic example of God speaking in pictures. Why does God speak in this way and how does it compare with Jesus speaking in parables?

CHAPTER 3

LOOKING AND LISTENING

This may sound strange, but a major part of listening to God is learning to look; and to look with understanding. This is something that only God can teach us, and our ability to look with understanding grows with spiritual maturity. We have already noted that the first essential is to learn to recognise when God is speaking to us and to be willing to listen. Once that willingness is established, being attentive to the Lord and listening for His voice becomes almost as natural as breathing. But it does take time, as well as a willing heart and an obedient spirit. We have to want to hear from God and make it our chief desire to seek Him with all our heart and mind and spirit. When we do so, we will certainly find Him, for that is His promise and God is always faithful to carry out His promises.

SIGHT AND SOUND
Looking and listening are closely related, just as sight and sound are related as the means by which we receive information from the world

around us. God uses the natural means of communication that He has given to all people as the means by which He communicates His Word. But our physical senses have to be sanctified by God for them to be effective channels through which He will communicate with us through His Holy Spirit. Our conversion experience should be enough for this sanctification to take place, but it is a fact that we live in an unholy world surrounded by unholy things and we are often pressurised by evil forces. We are constantly seeing and hearing things that are a denial of the sovereignty of God, and they seek to distract us from the fulfilment of His purposes for our lives.

The voices of the world are incessantly clamouring for our attention, and the values of the world distract us from the values of the Kingdom. Hence we are always in need of the renewing grace of God. We are all a bit like the leaky old water-butt we had in our garden in my childhood. There was a crack in the side several inches from the top which let the water drain out. A heavy rainfall during the night would fill the butt to the top, but during the day the water would leak out through the crack. It would never remain filled to the top. In the same way, we often start the day on a spiritual high, having had a good time of prayer during which we have truly experienced the presence of God. Then things happen during the day which sap our spiritual strength and by the evening we are desperately in need of a refilling of the Holy Spirit.

We constantly need to seek the forgiveness of God for the things we have done which are contrary to His will and the things that we have not done which we should have done. We need to seek forgiveness for the opportunities we have missed for bringing the Word of God into the lives of others – a word of comfort, rebuke, warning or guidance; above all, a winning word of love that the Father was longing to communicate to someone through us, but we were not listening or paying attention so the opportunity was missed.

WATCH AND PRAY

The Father wants us to be constantly alert, not simply so that He can speak to us for our own comfort and blessing but so that He can use us. We are not simply saved for ourselves; we are saved to serve. If we wish, when we reach the end of our earthly life, to hear the Master's voice saying, "Well done, good and faithful servant", we have to learn to be attentive to Him, which means learning to look as well as to listen. Just as God communicated with the prophets through sight as well as through sound and gave them spiritual discernment of the things that they were seeing, so He is longing to teach us to look with understanding. He expects those who are believers, especially those with leadership responsibilities, to be able to interpret what they are seeing.

I remember hearing Murray Watts recalling an amusing incident where he and a group of young people were going out to lead a Sunday evening service in a village somewhere outside York. They were standing at a bus stop in the city, growing increasingly anxious because the bus was late, and they were afraid that they would be late arriving for the evening service. One of them suggested that they should pray. So they all stood there fervently praying to the Lord to send the bus. While they were praying the bus came and swept past them because none of them had their eyes open to see the bus approaching and to request it to stop. Murray recalls this as a reminder that Jesus' instruction to His disciples was not just to pray, but to *watch* and pray!

In our times of intercession we should take with us what we have been observing in our daily lives. This means watching what is happening in the nation and in our local communities so that we can bring these things before the Lord, seeking both understanding and knowledge of what God is saying to us in current affairs as well as in our own personal circumstances. The Lord wants His people to be alert and well-informed so that we can be good witnesses, and in conversation with others we will be able rightly to apply the Word of God.

Jesus spoke severely to the Pharisees and Sadducees, the religious leaders of His own day, concerning their spiritual blindness. They came to Him asking for a sign from heaven.

> He replied, "When evening comes, you say, 'It will be fair weather, for the sky is red,' and in the morning, 'Today it will be stormy, for the sky is red and overcast.' You know how to interpret the appearance of the sky, but you cannot interpret the signs of the times. A wicked and adulterous generation looks for a miraculous sign, but none will be given it except the sign of Jonah." Jesus then left them and went away.
>
> (Matthew 16:1–4)

SIGN OF RESURRECTION

Jesus used a similar illustration about interpreting the weather when speaking not just to leaders but to a general crowd in Jerusalem. They were all Israelites, people in a covenant relationship with God, and therefore they should have been able to understand the significance of the times in which they were living. They had the Law and the Prophets to guide them. They were a people who had received the Word of the Lord as part of their history as well as through their religious heritage, and they should have been able to understand the way God was working out His purposes and therefore to interpret the signs of the times in their generation.

Addressing the crowd, Jesus said,

> When you see a cloud rising in the west, immediately you say, "It's going to rain," and it does. And when the south wind blows,

you say, "It's going to be hot," and it is. Hypocrites! You know how to interpret the appearance of the earth and the sky. How is it that you don't know how to interpret this present time?

(Luke 12:54–56)

Predicting the weather in Israel is, of course, not too difficult as a westerly wind coming off the Mediterranean usually means rain, whereas a south-easterly, coming off the desert, usually indicates a hot dry spell. The generation that witnessed the life and ministry of Jesus was privileged above all others. The men and women of that time saw things that the prophets had longed to see. Their religious leaders spent their lives studying the sacred writings of the Torah, the Prophets, the Talmud and the Babylonian Gemara, and teaching the people concerning the coming of Messiah.

They were experts on points of the Law and Messianic expectations, but when actually confronted with the evidence of Messiah's presence they were blind; so too were the people they taught. It is small wonder that Jesus wept when He surveyed the city of Jerusalem during the last week of His earthly ministry. He could already foresee the desolation of the city and the scattering into worldwide exile of the remnant of the people of Judea within the lifetime of many of those who were soon to call for His own crucifixion. The city and the people He loved were about to bring judgment upon themselves because of their blindness, because of their inability to interpret the signs of the times, because of their rejection of their own Messiah sent to them by the Father – in Jesus' own words this tragedy would happen "because you did not recognise the time of God's coming to you" (Luke 19:44).

BLIND WATCHMEN

The failure to look with understanding had always been responsible for the tragedies that had beset Israel throughout her history. Long before the time of Jesus, God had brought a similar charge against the religious leaders of the nation which is recorded in Isaiah 56:10–12:

> Israel's watchmen are blind,
>> they all lack knowledge.

(Isaiah 56:10)

The picture given here is of the watchmen patrolling the city walls whose task was to watch out for the first signs of danger so that they could blow the trumpet to warn the people and mobilise the defences to resist an attack, but the watchmen themselves were blind.

The city stood in greater danger than if they had no watchmen at all and everyone was keeping an eye open for danger. With "blind watchmen" upon the walls there was an atmosphere of complacency among the people as they believed they were safe and that they would be warned of approaching danger. It was, of course, inconceivable that the leaders of the nation would appoint blind men to be the city watchmen patrolling the walls. But Isaiah's charge was that the leaders themselves were spiritually blind, and therefore the leadership they were exercising was similar to that of blind watchmen who could not discern when to sound a warning to alert the people. The leaders of the nation were, he said, like "shepherds who lack understanding" (Isaiah 56:11). They said to each other,

> Tomorrow will be like today,
>> or even far better.

(Isaiah 56:12b)

Throughout the Bible, God's accusation is always sternest against those with leadership responsibilities. Those who exercise ministry among the people in the name of the Lord are accountable to God for the way they discharge those responsibilities. God made this clear to Ezekiel when he established the "watchman principle" that if the watchman does not give a clear warning to the people when he sees danger approaching, he himself will be held accountable for the disaster that overtakes the city. It was probably with this in mind that Jesus refused to give any further sign to the Pharisees and Sadducees who were the Lord's watchmen for the nation and who should have been able to interpret the signs of the times.

WATCHING THE FATHER

In His own ministry Jesus not only urged His followers to be a watching, praying people, but He Himself put this teaching into practice. His testimony was,

> The Son can do nothing by himself; he can do only what he sees his Father doing, because whatever the Father does the Son also does. For the Father loves the Son and shows him all he does . . .
>
> (John 5:19–20)

In the same context Jesus says,

> By myself I can do nothing; I judge only as I hear, and my judgment is just, for I seek not to please myself but him who sent me.
>
> (John 5:30)

These two statements in the same teaching discourse are important for understanding how Jesus Himself received revelation from the

Father. He says that what He receives from His Father comes from what He sees His Father doing and from what He hears God saying to Him. Seeing and hearing are thus central to the earthly ministry of Jesus. From our knowledge of the way the writing prophets of Israel exercised their ministry, we can see that this is exactly the same as the way they received their revelation and their understanding of the nature and purposes of God.

These two statements in John chapter 5 are of great importance in understanding the relationship between Jesus and His Father. The hallmark of Jesus' ministry was obedience to the Father. Many times He testified that He never did anything on His own initiative, that He could do nothing on His own. He continually emphasised His total dependence upon God for everything that He did and said. He emphasised that He only did those things which were pleasing to the Father. He said,

> I do nothing on my own but speak just what the Father has taught me. The one who sent me is with me; he has not left me alone, for I always do what pleases him.
>
> (John 8:28b–29)

Jesus' dependence upon His Father was so complete that even His body language and the intonation of His voice were directed through His intimate relationship with God. He said that the very words that He spoke were not His own but were given to Him, and He was shown exactly how to express the Word of God. He declared,

> For I did not speak of my own accord, but the Father who sent me commanded me what to say and how to say it . . . So whatever I say is just what the Father has told me to say.
>
> (John 12:49–50)

Jesus learned to watch and to listen. He watched and listened with understanding. He watched what the Father was actually doing. And many times He went away alone to have times of intercession, speaking with and listening to His Father. Of course, He had the advantage of having come from the Father and therefore knowing the Father's purposes from the beginning to the end. But during His earthly ministry He accepted the limitations of a human life, which necessitated spending considerable time in prayer to make sure that He was in full communion with God and understanding what His Father was doing from day to day and even from moment to moment as the time for His trial and crucifixion drew closer. For this reason He spent much of the final night with His disciples in the Garden of Gethsemane alone in prayer, returning to His disciples several times to ensure that they too were praying. Sadly their eyes were closed in sleep and their inner eyes were blinded to the significance of the events that were taking place around them.

Looking with understanding is of vital importance if we are to be a watching, praying people who understand the times in which we live, people who are able to declare the Word of God with authority to our generation. God has given us the ability to do this through giving us His Word in Scripture which enables us to know Him and to understand His purposes. In addition He has given us the same Holy Spirit poured out upon the first believers at Pentecost, which is still available to all those whose lives are committed to God the Father through the Lord Jesus, and who are obedient to His Word.

The Father wants us to be as the tribe of Issachar was to the nation of Israel in the time of King David. In 1 Chronicles 12 there is an account of a great coronation festival at Hebron when David became king in succession to Saul. Each of the tribes sent a contingent of fighting men, fully armed to support David. Verses 23–40 describe the numbers of the fully armed men from each of the tribes who "came to Hebron fully determined to make David king over all Israel" (verse 38) and the three days of the festival and feasting that followed. It is interesting to note that the only tribe not to send fighting men was the tribe of Issachar. Instead, they sent 200 of their leaders, "who understood the times and knew what Israel should do" (verse 32). Clearly, these were mature spiritual leaders who had learned to stand in the council of God. They must have been invaluable to David in the coming days. The following chapters record incidents in the history of the nation when there was an enemy threat and David "enquired of God" (1 Chronicles 14:10). At such times we may expect that the men of Issachar "who understood the times and knew what Israel should do" would have been among the king's counsellors.

Today God is looking for a people who understand the times and know what should be done by the people of God to fulfil the mission of Christ. That means learning not only to listen to God but also to look with understanding at what God is doing in the world and what He is allowing to happen in fulfilment of His purposes. Of course, to gain that understanding we have to be fully familiar with both the nature and the purposes of God as revealed to us in the Bible. We need to pay special attention to the teaching of Jesus and to the New Testament writers who were familiar with His teaching.

THE PROPHETIC METHOD

Strangely enough, the right method for understanding the times in which we live, and interpreting the signs, is not to begin with Biblical prophecies and then try to match them with events in the contemporary world. That is the method followed by the false teachers who play Bible mathematics and who try to forecast dates and times, which is expressly forbidden by Jesus (Acts 1:7).

The right method is always to follow that which was practised by the prophets. Their ministry always began with a personal experience of God. There is no substitute for this. Their deepest desire was to know God and always to please Him, being absolutely obedient to Him, taking time to learn to listen, to recognise His voice. Jesus had a similar desire of absolute obedience to His Father, which He expressed as doing nothing on His own initiative but doing and saying only what His Father directed. If Jesus recognised that He could do nothing on His own initiative, this should surely speak to us of our own dependence upon God, and that we should seek to do only those things which the Lord directs.

Long before the time of Jesus, the prophets had to learn their dependence upon God and only to speak when He told them to speak, and only to say what He told them to say; nothing more and nothing less. Once they had learned to listen, the prophets then learned to observe keenly, even noting the fine detail of contemporary events. Their next task was to get into the presence of the Lord and to seek His counsel. In their times of intercession they would spread before God the things they saw happening in the nation for which they were watchmen and intercessors. It was at these times that they received understanding, as God responded by giving them His Word concerning events in their day and revealing to them the outcome if the people continued along the path they were presently walking. When they stood in the council of the Lord the prophets were sometimes able to glimpse things that would happen far into the distant future as God revealed His overall purposes to them. The final task of the prophets was to declare the Word that God had given to them and the understanding He had revealed to them of the things that they were witnessing.

If we follow the same prophetic method today, we will note the great spiritual harvest that is taking place throughout the world as the Church worldwide is currently growing at a faster rate than at any time since the apostolic age. We will notice that the Spirit of God is being poured out primarily upon the humble poor in the developing nations rather than upon the peoples of the rich and powerful nations of the Western world. We will notice how all the nations of the world are being shaken in their economic, social and political systems and how many of the great empires of Mammon and man-made systems in which the nations put their trust are crumbling today. We will also notice how the forces of nature and natural processes are being shaken through extreme weather patterns, storms, droughts, floods, famines, plagues of locusts, strange diseases among cattle and incurable illnesses afflicting millions of people.

If we follow the prophetic method, having learned to get into the council of the Lord and to listen to His voice, we will take seriously our responsibility to be intercessors for the nations as well as watchmen. We will then spread this information before the Lord with open Bibles, seeking to understand what we are seeing in our own lifetime. It is then that the Spirit of the Living God enlightens our minds by bringing His Word to life and revealing to us the significance of the things we are seeing in our own lifetime. Looking and listening come together to produce a people like the tribe of Issachar who understand the times and know what should be done.

Questions

1. Matthew 16:1–4. The Pharisees were so absorbed with religious affairs that they failed to discern the signs of the times. Is that a danger for us today?

2. Is it too much to expect pastors to have prophetic insight? See Ephesians 1:11–16 and Numbers 11:24–30.

3. How important is it to have a worldwide perspective on what God is doing today rather than being familiar only with the local scene?

4. Luke 19:41–44. Why is a right discerning of the significance of the times in which we live important for intercession?

CHAPTER 4

LEARNING
TO LISTEN

Jesus was deeply committed to prayer. He regularly communicated with the Father, spending many hours talking with Him to ensure that He did only what His Father told Him to do. There are a number of references in the Gospels to Jesus going away privately to be alone in prayer. He not only got away from the crowds but He also left His own disciples so that He could be entirely alone with the Father. Mark records that at the very beginning of His ministry, immediately after He had spoken in the synagogue at Capernaum and healed Simon's mother- in-law, Jesus spent time in prayer:

> Very early in the morning, while it was still dark, Jesus got up, left the house and went off to a solitary place, where he prayed.
> (Mark 1:35)

Luke says that "Jesus often withdrew to lonely places and prayed" (Luke 5:16). It is also clear from the Gospel records that Jesus liked to go up into the hills, or even to climb a mountain, to find a suitable place for prayer. He liked not only to get away from people but also to get away from towns, buildings and anything man-made when He was seeking to get into the presence of the Father. Being high up in the hills of Galilee probably also enabled Him to overlook the towns and villages of the region, such as the village of Capernaum nestling on the shore of the Sea of Galilee where He had so many dear friends.

Spending time alone

Jesus' personal communication with the Father was so important to Him that He often got up very early in the morning before dawn to spend time quietly with the Father before beginning the day's ministry. This communication was essential in order for Him to know the will of the Father. Jesus' personal testimony was that He always did what was pleasing to the Father. He could only do this by doing nothing on His own initiative. Hence He was able to say,

> I do nothing on my own but speak just what the Father has taught me . . . for I always do what pleases him.
>
> (John 8:28b–29)

What a wonderful testimony it would be if we were able to say, "I only do what pleases God"! I personally don't know anyone who would dare to say such a thing. In fact, the closer we become in our walk with Jesus, the more we increase in spiritual maturity. But far from that bringing the confidence to say "I only do what pleases God", we are more likely to recognise our personal imperfections and our need for the forgiveness and grace of God.

The only way Jesus could be sure that He was only doing and saying what His Father told Him was to spend many hours in quietness listening to the Father and talking with Him. Before taking any major decision or new initiative in ministry, Jesus consulted His Father. In the early days of His ministry He had many disciples following Him but there came a point when He wished to choose twelve who would be His close companions; these men would become the apostles who were sent out to take the message to the nations after He returned to the Father. Such a major decision required extra-careful checking with the Father, so in this case Jesus did not simply get up early in the morning to pray but spent the whole night in prayer. Luke records,

> One of those days Jesus went out to a mountainside to pray, and spent the night praying to God. When morning came, he called his disciples to him and chose twelve of them, whom he also designated apostles.
>
> (Luke 6:12–13)

It was Jesus' personal example of His own commitment to prayer that caused the disciples to ask Him to teach them how to pray. Luke again records,

> One day Jesus was praying in a certain place. When he finished, one of his disciples said to him, "Lord, teach us to pray, just as John taught his disciples."
>
> (Luke 11:1)

After teaching them what we know as "The Lord's Prayer", Jesus went on to speak to them about persistence in intercession. But a major part of Jesus' teaching on prayer is found, not in the Synoptic Gospels but in the Gospel of John, who remembered Jesus' emphasis upon listening.

THE SHEPHERD AND THE SHEEP

In chapter 10 of his Gospel, John records Jesus' use of the description of the relationship between the shepherd and his sheep. The significance of this can only be appreciated if it is understood in the context of methods of sheep rearing and tending in Israel. These methods have not changed much since the time of Jesus 2,000 years ago and can still be seen today. They contrast starkly with modern Western methods of sheep farming. In the West we are used to enclosed fields and absent shepherds. This is so different that the message Jesus was conveying to His disciples can easily be missed. In the West the shepherd only occasionally visits his sheep, and when he does so, he often uses a dog to round them up and then drives them from behind. The sheep obey because they are afraid of the dog and the man driving them.

In Israel the same methods of sheep farming can be seen today as were familiar in the time of Jesus. The shepherd goes ahead of his flock, searching out good pasture and watching over his flock every hour of the day. This was clearly the experience of the young boy David, son of Jesse, who was sent into the fields to guard the family flock. He knew what it was to be responsible for the safety of the sheep when they were attacked by wild animals. It was this experience that later gave him the confidence in God to face Israel's enemies. His personal experience of the presence of God as he guided the sheep is to be seen in the words of Psalm 23 which speak of the way God leads His people along safe pathways and to fertile fields. The shepherd would always go ahead of his flock, watching out for danger. He would protect the flock from wild animals even at the risk of his own life. As Jesus said, a good shepherd would be prepared to lay down his life for the sheep whereas mere hired hands who had no real commitment to the sheep would run away in the face of danger and leave the wolf to savage the flock. It may be because Western Christians have never really understood Eastern methods of sheep farming that some churches have introduced a type of pastoral care, or "shepherding", that is oppressive rather than enabling. Some leaders have misinterpreted the role of the shepherd in terms of an authoritarian leader driving the sheep, rather than one who serves by enduring every kind of hardship, even to the point of sacrificing his own self-interest for the well-being of the sheep.

At night, a number of shepherds used to come together, leading their flocks into an enclosure where they would be secure against attack. The gate would be closed and a watchman would be placed on duty while the other shepherds slept on the open hillside – around a fire during the cold winter nights. In the morning, the shepherds would go in turn to the enclosure. The watchman recognised each one and opened the gate. The shepherd would only have to stand there and call. His own sheep would separate themselves from the others belonging to other flocks and would come to him. He would move off and they would follow him. The sheep recognised the voice of their own shepherd because they spent so many hours with him. Throughout the day he would speak to them so they became familiar with every tone in his voice. When he warned of danger approaching they recognised his call, and the stragglers would hurry to come close to him. If he wished to turn to the left or to the right, he would only have to speak to them and they would follow him. Jesus said,

My sheep listen to my voice; I know them, and they follow me.
(John 10:27)

It was because the sheep were so familiar with the voice of their own shepherd that they were able to recognise his voice among all the voices of the other shepherds. And it was because a relationship of trust had been built up between the shepherd and the sheep that they responded immediately when he spoke. Theirs was not an unwilling obedience born out of fear or of being driven; it was the willing obedience of knowing that the shepherd served their own best interests, that he loved them, protected them and provided for them.

RECOGNISING THE VOICE OF JESUS

In using the illustration of the shepherd and his flock in John 10, Jesus clearly intended his followers to have the same love and trust for Him and to become so familiar with His voice that they would respond instantly when He spoke to them. For the first disciples this was relatively easy because they spent many hours talking with Jesus as they walked from town to town and village to village in Galilee and Judea. They accompanied Him on the long trek up to Jerusalem from Galilee via the Decapolis, preaching among the Gentiles in their cities, crossing the Jordan and facing the long climb up from Jericho to the hills surrounding Jerusalem, through the friendly village of Bethany and over the Mount of Olives into the city. On these long walks Jesus would have spent a great deal of time talking to His disciples about the Kingdom of God and teaching them about the mission upon which they would soon be embarking. He prepared them by sending them out in small groups. On one occasion seventy-two were sent on a mission and came back rejoicing at the many things God had done through them.

It was this personal contact with Jesus throughout the years of His active ministry from the time of His baptism by John that created a deep spiritual relationship with His disciples, who were later to become the apostles and leaders of the early Church. They became so familiar with Him, seeing at first hand the power of God as He ministered to the sick and as He reached the crowds, that even when they were not with Him they would be conscious of His presence when they were ministering to others, and they would remember His teaching and the parables He used.

The disciples spent many hours in the presence of Jesus, listening to His voice, so that after the crucifixion and resurrection they were so familiar with His voice that later on they would know when He was speaking to them. They were able to recognise Him in His resurrection appearances when they heard His voice calling to them from the shore of the Sea of Galilee when they were fishing, even though in the early morning mist they did not recognise His appearance. As soon as He spoke to them and told them where to direct their nets they knew it was Jesus (John 21:4–7). When Jesus finally ascended to the Father and no longer appeared to them in person, they had become so used to His appearances and they were so familiar with His voice that it no longer mattered that His physical presence had been withdrawn. They had that strong sense of Jesus being with them, alongside them or ahead of them, wherever they went and at all times of day or night. He had taught them how to pray and to get into the presence of the Father as He had done throughout His ministry, so they simply followed the same practice, continuing as He had taught them whilst He was physically with them.

For those who want to be His close disciples today, it is possible to become really familiar with the voice of Jesus by reading the Gospels regularly and becoming familiar with the things Jesus did and said. Shortly before the crucifixion, Jesus prayed not only for the first generation of believers but for all those who would believe through their witness. He concluded his prayer with the words,

I have made you known to them, and will continue to make you known in order that the love you have for me may be in them and that I myself may be in them.

(John 17:26)

Jesus also promised, when He gave the Great Commission for the gospel to be carried to all nations throughout the world, that He would be with those who are His disciples wherever they go until the end of time.

If we wish to know Jesus and to hear His voice clearly today, we have to learn to be quiet, to be still and know the presence of God. This means learning how and when to block out the world. Just as Jesus went alone up into the hills of Galilee to pray, so we need times when we are completely alone if we are to learn to stand in the council of God.

PERCEPTION

The prophets knew by experience that God could speak to them in many ways and at any time of day or night. God could use the things they were seeing and experiencing in order to convey a message to them. Jeremiah was probably out walking when he saw an almond tree and immediately heard the voice of the Lord coming into his mind and dropping a message into his spirit using a Hebrew pun, because "watching" and "almond tree" sound the same in that language. As he looked at the tree he heard God's voice:

"What do you see, Jeremiah?"
"I see the branch of an almond tree," I replied.
The LORD said to me, "You have seen correctly, for I am *watching* to see that my word is fulfilled."

(Jeremiah 1:11–12; my emphasis)

On another occasion God used an ordinary everyday scene to impress upon the prophet the necessity of learning to watch as well as to pray. Jeremiah was told to go to the potter's shop and watch:

> Go down to the potter's house, and there I will give you my message.
>
> (Jeremiah 18:2)

This was a strange instruction and Jeremiah had no idea what was going to happen and why he had been given such an instruction. But he obeyed because God had spoken to him saying, "There I will give you my message." He went, and stood there watching the potter at work.

Jeremiah was probably quite familiar with the potter and had no doubt watched him at work many times. Probably he asked him what he was making and watched the man struggle to form a beautiful vase. But all his skill was to no avail. He was working with an unresponsive piece of clay that simply would not run in his hands. Eventually the potter abandoned the task and patiently put the crushed lump of clay back onto the wheel and reshaped it into a different pot which would not be the original thing of beauty he had planned, but would be a useful vessel that would serve a housewife in her kitchen.

Jeremiah instantly perceived the significance of this in terms of God's patience with His people. It is more than possible that when the potter abandoned all hope of fashioning the vessel of his choice, Jeremiah expected to see him crush the obstinate clay in his hand and fling it across the floor of the potter's shop. But instead of discarding the clay, he patiently put it back onto the wheel and set about the task of making it into a new pot. The potter's action spoke strongly to Jeremiah of God's willingness to forgive the obstinacy of His people which was preventing Him from working out His good plans for the whole nation. It was here in the potter's shop that God gave to Jeremiah a message concerning His love and forgiveness and how He longed to work out His plans not only for Israel but for all the nations of the world if only they would turn to Him, listen to His voice and obey His Word.

There is nowhere else in Scripture that gives a clearer message, not simply to Israel, but to the nations of the world:

> If at any time I announce that a nation or kingdom is to be uprooted, torn down and destroyed, and if that nation I warned repents of its evil, then I will relent and not inflict on it the disaster I had planned. And if at another time I announce that a nation or kingdom is to be built up and planted, and if that nation does evil in my sight and does not obey me, then I will reconsider the good I had intended to do for it.
>
> (Jeremiah 18:7–10)

God is still conveying the same message to His people today – to all who will listen to His Word. But we are a stubborn and rebellious people in the same mould as His people Israel in the time of Jeremiah. We do not learn from the lessons of the past; so the tragedies of history are repeated in successive generations. But God is patient, loving and forgiving; more ready to forgive and to restore than we are to repent and to turn to Him. The key to obedience and trust in the Lord lies in our learning to listen and to recognise His voice.

QUESTIONS

1. Luke 5:16. Why did Jesus spend so much time in prayer?
2. John 10:1–18. What does this teach us about the nature and purposes of God?

3. John 20:10–18. Mary recognised the voice of Jesus when He spoke her name. How do you recognise the voice of Jesus?

4. Isaiah 50:4–5. What is special about the early morning for listening to God?

CHAPTER 5

LISTENING AND OBEYING

On numerous occasions throughout His ministry Jeremiah pleaded with the people to listen to the Word of God. Their apparent deafness brought great sorrow to the prophet, not simply because his warnings went unheeded and he himself was rejected, scorned and often physically abused, but because he already foresaw the consequences of the nation's stubborn refusal to heed the warnings God was sending them. He told the people:

> If you do not listen,
>   I will weep in secret
>   because of your pride;
> my eyes will weep bitterly,
>   overflowing with tears,
>   because the LORD's flock will be taken captive.
>
> (Jeremiah 13:17)

God could hardly have warned the nation more clearly than he did through Jeremiah:

> Therefore, this is what the LORD God Almighty, the God of Israel, says: "Listen! I am going to bring on Judah and on everyone living in Jerusalem every disaster I pronounced against them. I spoke to them, but they did not listen; I called to them, but they did not answer."
>
> (Jeremiah 35:17)

It was not as though God was only just beginning to speak to them for the first time in their history. More than a hundred years before Jeremiah, the prophet Amos had brought strong warnings to the northern kingdom of Israel. He said,

> Surely the eyes of the Sovereign LORD
>   are on the sinful kingdom.
> I will destroy it
>   from the face of the earth . . .
> For I will give the command,
>   and I will shake the house of Israel
>   among all the nations
> as grain is shaken in a sieve . . .
>
> (Amos 9:8–9)

The history of Israel was studded with stubborn disobedience and a refusal to listen to God. As the day of Jerusalem's destruction drew nearer during the ministry of Jeremiah, God's warnings through him became more urgent. He was instructed to say,

This is what the LORD says: If you do not listen to me and follow my law, which I have set before you, and if you do not listen to the words of my servants the prophets, whom I have sent to you again and again (though you have not listened), then I will make this house like Shiloh and this city an object of cursing among all the nations of the earth.

(Jeremiah 26:4–6)

HEEDING THE WORD OF GOD

God always has a purpose in speaking to us. His Word does not return to Him empty. It accomplishes His purpose. But it can only do so if we are listening and taking notice of Him in our lives, and listening with an obedient spirit. It is not enough simply to listen; we have to listen and *heed* the Word of the Lord. In the last chapter we were speaking about the necessity of learning to listen, but we will never learn to listen until we *want* to listen. And wanting to listen must not be out of a mere sense of curiosity, a desire to possess supernatural knowledge, or to have the future revealed to us. There has to be a real desire to obey the will of God, a spirit of willing obedience. Otherwise, God, who knows the heart of each of His children, most certainly will not reveal His Word to us. If our heart attitude towards God is right then our chief desire will be to hear from Him, because we know that He has good plans for us, plans for our good and not for our harm, because He loves us. The key to listening with the right attitude lies in our relationship with God, which is based upon the recognition of His love that enables us to trust Him completely. Then when we hear His Word, we respond with willing obedience, because we know that when we do so, all things will work together for our good.

The prophets learned the necessity for absolute obedience when handling the Word of the Lord. They probably all knew the story of the unnamed prophet in 1 Kings 13 who was sent by God with a message for King Jeroboam which he had to deliver at Bethel. It was not very far from Judah to Bethel in Israel which was only about ten miles north of Jerusalem. The prophet was told by the Lord,

> You must not eat bread or drink water or return by the way you came.
>
> (1 Kings 13:9)

So after delivering the warning message of judgment and refusing food and drink at the sanctuary, the prophet "took another road and did not return by the way he had come to Bethel" (13:10).

On the return journey an old man claiming to be a prophet met him and countermanded the Word of the Lord, saying that God had told him to offer hospitality to the young prophet on his return journey to Judah. The young prophet fell for this deception and during the meal the old man cried out,

> This is what the LORD says: "You have defied the word of the LORD and have not kept the command the LORD your God gave you. You came back and ate bread and drank water in the place where he told you not to eat or drink. Therefore your body will not be buried in the tomb of your fathers."
>
> (1 Kings 13:21–22)

If he had been in a right relationship with God he would have been listening and would have heard God's warning. Within a few hours this prophecy was tragically fulfilled when the young prophet was mauled by a lion and killed on the final part of his journey back home.

Many Christians find this account of the fate of the disobedient prophet difficult to accept because it does not fit comfortably with the New Testament revelation of God. They argue that Jesus taught His disciples to know God as a loving, forgiving Father who would not set a lion on one of His faithful servants who had been hoodwinked by a deceiver. But this is to miss the point. Of course, God does not deliberately send punishment upon His servants. But He knew what would happen to this young man if He travelled that road at that time. He warned him, but the warning was ignored. We all live in a sinful world full of threats to our safety and well-being. The sun and the rain fall upon the just and the unjust. We are all constantly surrounded by danger. When we are deliberately disobedient, as this young prophet was, and we do something God has expressly forbidden, we put ourselves outside the protection of God. Time and again the history of Israel reflects this, both in God's dealing with individuals and with the nation as a whole.

HOLINESS IS SEPARATION

God looks for obedience in all His children, which is for our good. But for those who seek to stand in His council and to hear Him speak there is an additional requirement, of both holiness and obedience. The holiness required by the Lord is that of *separation from the world*; not a physical separation but a *spiritual* separation. None of the prophets of Israel lived the life of a recluse. They were constantly among the people, in the city streets and market squares, and travelling through the towns and villages of the countryside. But all the people knew that the prophets were different; they were different in their lifestyle, but most of all, there was a spiritual difference, an intangible, indefinable spiritual charisma that marked each of the prophets as a man or woman of God. It was said of Moses that when he came down from the mountain his face shone with a brilliance that caused those around him to fear even to look at him. They knew that he had been in the presence of the Living God.

It was this awesomeness of the presence of God that somehow surrounded the prophets that was responsible for saving their lives on more than one occasion. Even evil and violent men feared to stretch out their hands against the Lord's anointed servants. The reason why the prophets were shown such respect, even by those who hated their message and desired above all things to silence them, was because the prophets obeyed God even in the smallest detail. That obedience was clear for all to see. Ezekiel was once told by God not to speak the Word of the Lord to the elders of Israel when they came enquiring for guidance. God warned him that if he was persuaded to utter a prophecy when the Lord had forbidden him to speak, God would stretch out his hand against him and destroy him (Ezekiel 14:9). His disobedience would make him as rebellious as the people to whom he was supposed to be ministering:

> The prophet will be as guilty as the one who consults him.
>
> (Ezekiel 14:10b)

ABSOLUTE OBEDIENCE

God requires a special obedience from those who seek to come into His presence and to hear His Word. It is a question of commitment. If we really wish to hear from Him then we have to be prepared to accept the responsibility that goes with the Word of the Lord. This was never a comfortable task for the prophets whose obedience must often have been strained almost to breaking point by the tasks they were given to do. Micah was told to wail; to go about barefoot and naked; to howl like a jackal; to moan like an owl and actually to roll naked in the dust of the streets of Jerusalem (Micah 1:8–11). Ezekiel was told to dress up like a refugee and to pack his belongings onto his back as though he were leaving the city for a long journey by foot (Ezekiel 12). Jeremiah was told to buy a pot and to take the city elders out to the Valley of Ben Hinnom and smash the jar in their presence (Jeremiah 19:1–10). But the prophets were never simply told to do something for no purpose. Each of them was given a message appropriate to the action they had to undertake. Jeremiah had to say,

> This is what the LORD Almighty says: I will smash this nation and this city just as this potter's jar is smashed and cannot be repaired.
>
> (Jeremiah 19:11)

God's requirement of absolute obedience is unwavering for those who claim to be His servants and who wish to hear from Him.

When we listen to the Lord and hear Him speaking to us we do not always receive the complete message at that time. God does not always reveal the end from the beginning. He often reveals only a small part. This is partly in order to protect us because we might shrink back in fear at the enormity of the task before us if we saw the whole purpose of God from the beginning. It also acts as a test of obedience. God gives us just a small part of the task to accomplish and when we have faithfully carried that out, he will give us the next step.

There are many examples of this in the Bible such as when Jeremiah was told to go and buy a linen belt and put it around his waist (Jeremiah 13:1). He did this and was then told,

> Take the belt you bought and are wearing round your waist, and go now to Perath and hide it there in a crevice in the rocks.
>
> (Jeremiah 13:4)

He did this also, and many days later God spoke to him again, telling him to go and recover the belt, which was now so rotted that it was completely useless. It was only at this point that the message came to Jeremiah:

> This is what the LORD says: "In the same way I will ruin the pride of Judah and the great pride of Jerusalem. These wicked people, who refuse to listen to my words, who follow the stubbornness of their hearts and go after other gods to serve and worship them, will be like this belt – completely useless!"
>
> (Jeremiah 13:9–10)

THE FAITHFULNESS OF GOD

Another reason why we need to learn the discipline of obedience if we are to hear from the Lord is because God is a God of detail and perfect timing in His Word. He does not just speak in vague terms. When He reveals a Word to His servants it is with accuracy, and if we respond rightly, we will discover the perfect timing of our God. He often leaves us until the last moment, to the fifty-ninth minute of the eleventh hour. But God is faithful to carry out His Word. If we are sure we have heard Him rightly, we can stand upon that Word with absolute confidence. In our own lives, my wife and I have proved this many times.

In 1972, when our ministry was serving a group of churches in the East End of London, a neighbouring church was declared "redundant" and was to be sold. Like so many other churches in our area it would have become either a supermarket or a mosque.

We got before the Lord in prayer and were very clearly told to buy it and that it would become a centre of evangelism and outreach for the gospel into our multiracial community. We had no money but we made an offer for it, which after prolonged negotiation was accepted. We still had no money when the contracts arrived for signature. We made no public appeal because the Lord had said He would supply the funds.

The day before the legal deadline, we called our people to a day of prayer and earnest intercession. We cried out to the Lord to fulfil His promise to us. The next morning, almost literally at the last minute on the last day, a man telephoned to say he had heard of the work we were doing and was there anything he could do to help? Half-jokingly I replied, "Yes, you can buy us a church!" There was a long pause before he said, "How much money do you need?" I told him the figure and to my amazement he said he would give us the whole amount plus an additional sum to support the work. God's timing often tests our faith to the limit, but He will always fulfil His promises to us.

REVELATION AND INTERCESSION

Listening and obedience take on a new significance when applied to intercession and spiritual warfare. If you get into intercession without first seeking the Lord for guidance, you have no idea what is on the Father's heart so you may, in fact, be asking for things that are contrary to the will of God. For example, in Jeremiah's time there were many false prophets who were declaring a message of peace. They were actually putting themselves against God by saying, "Peace! Peace!" whereas God was saying, "There is no peace."

Jeremiah stated,

The prophet who prophesies peace will be recognised as one truly sent by the LORD only if his prediction comes true.

(Jeremiah 28:9)

In the time of Elijah there were plenty of false prophets who were interceding for rain during the three-and-a-half years' drought. Their prayers were not answered because they were not praying within the will of the Father. God had told Elijah to declare a drought because of the stubbornness of the people. There would be no rain until the people turned away from listening to the prophets of Baal and practising idolatry. After the contest on Mount Carmel and the destruction of the false prophets, God told Elijah that the rain would come. It was then that Elijah got to his knees and cried out to the Lord for the rain to start. His task was to pray into being upon earth the thing that he had heard in the heavenlies. He could pray now with absolute confidence because he had heard the Father declare that the time had come for the drought to be broken. Elijah was therefore able to intercede with absolute confidence, knowing that he was praying in the will of the Father. Elijah's confidence in the Lord was so great that he was able to tell Ahab to get off the mountain and go home because heavy rain was on its way. He declared this even before he got into intercession for the rain to come.

The most effective form of prayer is intercession combined with revelation. When we have spent time listening to the Lord and we know what is on the Father's heart, we are able to pray with the absolute confidence of knowing that our prayers will be answered. If we pray for things that are simply our own good ideas we may even put ourselves against God. For example, if God is saying, "I am shaking the nation" and we pray "O God, stop shaking the nation; please put the economy right and give us social or political stability", we would then be praying directly contrary to the will of God. We need to ask the Lord why He is shaking the nation; then our prayers change to: "O God, make the shaking of the nation effective so that You may accomplish Your purposes and carry out Your good plans for the nation."

Even when we are praying for ourselves or for other individuals we should first seek to know what is on the Father's heart so that we can pray with confidence. Once we know we have heard from Him, we are under an obligation to obey. The right response may be to get into intercession or it may be that the Father is calling for some action. Whatever is appropriate, the first essential is to learn to listen carefully to the Lord; then we can follow the instruction given by Mary the mother of Jesus to the servants at the wedding in Cana in Galilee:

Do whatever he tells you.

(John 2:5)

QUESTIONS

1. Kings 13. Why was it of such vital importance for the prophet to learn absolute obedience to God?

2. How can we improve our attentiveness and obedience to God?

3. See 2 Chronicles 18:1–27. The Old Testament prophets were lonely figures but under the New Covenant we are members of a Body. How should those receiving prophetic revelation submit to one another in the context of 1 Corinthians 12 and 14?

4. Discuss the relation between revelation and intercession.

CHAPTER 6

HOW TO LISTEN

The Westminster Confession states that the chief object of the Christian faith is "to know God and to enjoy him for ever". It is this fundamental quest for God that is the chief end of humankind. It is the primary purpose of life, underlying God's creation of men and women in His own image. "Our souls are restless until they find their rest in God," said Augustine. The quest of the true believer is in seeking God for Himself, not for any reward or personal advancement, but simply in order to know Him and to enjoy being in His presence; to know Him more clearly and to love Him more dearly. The love of God creates a desire within the true believer to be close to Him in the same way as we want to be close to the person most loved in our lives, and just as we want to do things to please our loved one, so we want our lives to be pleasing to God.

SEEKING THE FACE OF GOD
Seeking the face of God begins as a desire of the heart, but it

is accomplished *as an act of will*. The psalmist summarises this beautifully when he says,

> My heart says of you, "Seek his face!"
>> Your face, LORD, I will seek.

> (Psalm 27:8)

The Pentateuch on many occasions refers to the intimate relationship between Moses and God:

> The LORD would speak to Moses face to face, as a man speaks with his friend.

> (Exodus 33:11a)

But this does not mean that Moses actually saw the face of God with his physical eyesight. Jesus stated quite categorically that He was the only one who had ever seen the Father:

> No-one has seen the Father except the one who is from God; only he has seen the Father.

> (John 6:46)

Yet God Himself gave a clear commandment to Solomon that he and all the Lord's people should seek His face. The words of 2 Chronicles 7:14 are often quoted today but they were well known in ancient Israel as a command particularly applicable to times of national disaster. God had said to Solomon that in such times,

> If my people, who are called by my name, will humble themselves and pray and *seek my face* and turn from their wicked ways, then

will I hear from heaven and will forgive their sin and will heal their land.

(2 Chronicles 7:14; my emphasis)

From the time of Moses, throughout the history of Israel, it was recognised that the greatest blessing flowed to individuals and to the nation when the face of God was turned towards the people. Conversely, when God turned His face away, the consequences were terrible. In many of the Psalms the question is asked, Why has God turned His face away from the people? Typical is Psalm 44:24:

Why do you hide your face
and forget our misery and oppression?

But the psalmist also recognises the connection between being in a right relationship with God and seeing His face:

For the LORD is righteous,
he loves justice;
upright men will see his face.

(Psalm 11:7)

The psalmist nevertheless pleads,

How long will you hide your face from me?

(Psalm 13:1b)

The answer to the divine dilemma posed by God's justice and His mercy is given by Isaiah through whom God says,

"In a surge of anger
    I hid my face from you for a moment,
but with everlasting kindness
    I will have compassion on you,"
says the LORD your Redeemer.

(Isaiah 54:8)

Ezekiel received a similar word:

The people of Israel went into exile for their sin, because they
were unfaithful to me. So I hid my face from them and handed
them over to their enemies . . .

(Ezekiel 39:23)

But in His compassion God eventually heeded the cries of His
people and moved to accomplish their restoration. He declared,

I will no longer hide my face from them, for I will pour out my
Spirit on the house of Israel, declares the Sovereign LORD.

(Ezekiel 39:29)

Hosea was probably the first to perceive what we have called the
"divine dilemma" when he referred to the great love of God for
Israel despite their unfaithfulness. In the presence of the Lord he
heard God saying,

How can I give you up, Ephraim?
    How can I hand you over, Israel?

(Hosea 11:8)

Gradually, through the unfolding history of Israel, there is revealed the same process that was repeated time after time of God establishing His covenant relationship with the people, only to see that relationship being broken through sin and faithlessness, which was then followed by punishment under which the nation cried out to the Lord for mercy. This was followed by His forgiveness, restoration and a time of blessing, until greed, selfishness and the spiritual short-sightedness of the people and their leaders started the whole process over again. The tragedy of the history of Israel is summarised in this word of the Lord to Hosea:

> When I fed them, they were satisfied;
>> when they were satisfied, they became proud;
> then they forgot me.

(Hosea 13:6)

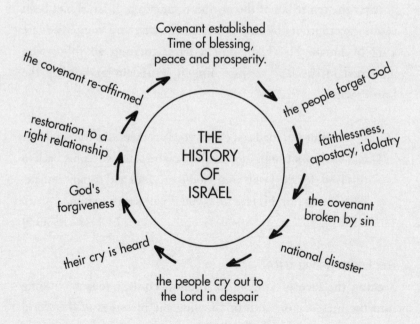

The history of Israel reads like a constantly revolving cycle. When the people were faithful and put their trust in God and were obedient to His Word, they enjoyed peace and prosperity. But they soon became lax, forgot God, and turned to other gods – with tragic results. This circle of judgment and blessing is illustrated in the diagram.

It is the deep desire of God's heart that His people should not seek Him only when everything is going wrong. This would turn our relationship with God into a kind of lifeboat situation, for emergency use only; we only entrust ourselves to it when the ship is sinking and all other hope is gone. Yet this is how so many people regard their relationship with the Father. They say, "Everything possible has been done. The only hope now is prayer!" God is looking for a people who will seek Him for Himself and for no other reason.

After the ten tribes of the northern kingdom of Israel had been taken into captivity by the Assyrians, the wise and compassionate king of Judah, Hezekiah, sent a letter inviting all those who remained in the land to join him in Jerusalem to worship the Lord, saying,

> If you return to the LORD, then your brothers and your children will be shown compassion by their captors and will come back to this land, for the LORD your God is gracious and compassionate. He will not turn his face from you if you return to him.
>
> (2 Chronicles 30:9)

RECEIVING REVELATION

Seeking the face of God in its Biblical context means entering into the presence of God, or allowing the pressures of the world to drop away so that there may be an increased awareness of the presence of God. Through prayer and meditation the point may be reached where the things of the world have dropped completely out of the conscious mind so that the spirit is free to be in intimate communion with the Spirit of God. Solitude is usually essential, and meditating upon a particular passage of Scripture helps to concentrate the mind upon some particular aspect of the nature and purposes of God that helps to draw the believer into a heightened awareness of His presence. It is at such times that we are open to receive divine revelation. It is at this point that we need to know how to recognise and to interpret what God is communicating to us.

Perhaps the best illustration of receiving divine revelation is that of a radio or television receiver. The airwaves are full of signals, both audio and video that, when unscrambled from their carrier waves, will give meaningful sounds or pictures. But the audio and vision receivers have to be correctly tuned, as well as being capable of interpreting the signals received. If the receivers are not tuned in to the correct frequency they will receive nothing, or will possibly even receive signals from an alien source. If the receiver is correctly tuned to the right station it will receive the desired sound or picture. It will, of course, only receive the sound or picture if it is in good working order, and if the power is switched on! The parallel of our receiving from God through the power of the Holy Spirit should be obvious.

God communicates with us through both sound and vision. Numbers 12:6–8 refers to three ways in which God communicates with us:

> When a prophet of the LORD is among you,
> > I reveal myself to him in visions,
> > I speak to him in dreams.

But this is not true of my servant Moses;
    he is faithful in all my house.
With him I speak face to face,
    clearly and not in riddles . . .

Throughout the Bible there are many examples of God communicating with men or women through one or other of these three ways. Apart from Daniel there is no evidence that the Biblical prophets received their messages through dreams. And the book of Daniel is not listed among the Prophets in the Hebrew Bible. It is found among the Wisdom literature.

Usually God either spoke directly to the prophets by bringing words into their minds together with the instruction as to what they were to do with it, or He communicated through pictures. These occurred either through a picture being formed in the mind of the prophet or through seeing something through which a message was conveyed. The picture required interpretation, but usually its meaning was clear. It is only in apocalyptic prophecy that we find symbols being used that required specialised interpretation. Such prophecy usually occurred during times of persecution so that if the record of it fell into the hands of the enemy no harm would be done, because only the people of God knew the code that enabled them to interpret the message.

God does not normally speak in code. He is a loving Father who does not wish to make it difficult for His children to understand Him. There has been a lot of confusion over this in recent times because of the misunderstanding of tongues. Paul says quite clearly that tongues are *to* God whereas messages (prophecies) are *from* God. The latter are in plain everyday language (1 Corinthians 14).

Jesus received instruction from the Father, just as the prophets did, through sight and sound. His testimony in John chapter 5 makes this clear. He said,

> The Son can do nothing by himself; he can do only what he *sees* his Father doing, because whatever the Father does the Son also *does*. For the Father loves the Son and shows him all he does . . .
>
> By myself I can do nothing; I judge only as I *hear*, and my judgment is just, for I seek not to please myself but him who sent me.
>
> (John 5:19–20, 30; my emphasis)

The unchangeable God, who is the same yesterday, today and for ever, still communicates with His children in the same way as He communicated with the prophets of ancient Israel and with His own beloved Son – through sight and sound, through pictures and through words. He does this in the same way as He has always communicated with those who have eyes to see and ears to hear, by bringing His Word into their conscious mind through the activity of the Holy Spirit within the spirit of man, so that it can be understood with the mind and perceived and acted upon.

STANDING IN THE COUNCIL OF THE LORD

It is not only leaders and those with ministry gifts who can hear from the Lord. Any Spirit-filled believer can receive divine revelation. This does not mean that everyone has the ministry of the prophet. Very, very few are called to such a ministry. In the whole of the New Testament there are only four who are named as having the ministry of the prophet; this involved them, for example Agabus, in a full-time itinerant ministry, travelling from place to place and region to region bringing the Word of God to the churches.

What we are emphasising is that every true believer who has received the Spirit of God and is in a right relationship with the Father through the precious blood of the Lord Jesus Christ is able to hear from God and to receive guidance for their own life, or for others close to them in the family or the local fellowship of believers. This fulfils the desire expressed by Moses:

> I wish that all the LORD's people were *prophets* and that the LORD would put his Spirit on them!
>
> (Numbers 11:29b; my emphasis)

Many years later God promised to make this possible:

> I will pour out my Spirit on your offspring,
>   and my blessing on your descendants.
>
> (Isaiah 44:3b)

But it was Joel who actually prophesied the events that took place at Pentecost when the Spirit of God was poured out upon young and old, men and women, rich and poor, and all believers were given the power to hear from God and to declare His Word. This is precisely what Peter meant when he told the crowd in Jerusalem that "they will prophesy" (Acts 2:18).

Hearing from God, in prophetic language, is what Jeremiah described as "standing in the council of the Lord". Of the false prophets he asked,

> Which of them has stood in the council of the LORD
>   to see or to hear his word?
>
> (Jeremiah 23:18)

Learning to listen to God as the prophets did, and as believers did in the New Testament Church, requires an act of will that translates a desire into a determination to seek and to find. Through Jeremiah God promised,

> "You will call upon me and come and pray to me, and I will listen to you. You will seek me and find me when you seek me with all your heart. I will be found by you," declares the LORD.
>
> (Jeremiah 29:12–14)

Hearing from God is not just a haphazard occurrence. It often takes years of dedicated constant seeking to learn how to get into the presence of the Living God who is found only by those who approach Him with "reverence and awe" (Hebrews 12:28).

Even when we discover the secret of getting into the presence of God through seeking His face, it is not automatic that we will hear from Him. Standing in the council of God requires something additional in intercession and quiet submissive obedience. When we stand in the council of God it is something similar to citizens exercising their right to sit in the public gallery overlooking the City Council Chamber and listen to the elected elders of the community speaking about matters concerning the life of the city. The citizen is permitted to sit there quietly, listening to the deliberations of the city councillors.

When we enter the council of the Lord it is as though we are hearing the deliberations of Father, Son and Holy Spirit and seeking to know what the Father and the Son are conveying to the people through the Holy Spirit.

Sometimes we seek to get into the presence of God for guidance on a specific issue, as King David did on one occasion:

During the reign of David, there was a famine for three successive years; so David sought the face of the Lord.

(2 Samuel 21:1a)

But guidance does not necessarily come quickly or easily; sometimes it is the result of a prolonged period of intercession, as was the case with Jeremiah when he was asked by the remnant who survived the Babylonian massacre whether they should stay in the land or flee to Egypt. It took Jeremiah ten days of fervent intercession, standing in the council of the Lord, before he could be sure that he had got the right answer and was able to give it to the people with confidence (Jeremiah 42:7).

No one should think that standing in the council of the Lord is either easy or automatic. It begins with seeking the face of God, and then through earnest intercession and quiet waiting we learn to get into His council and to receive His Word. There is no set rule regarding the best time or method. Each person has to find his or her own way to the Father. For Isaiah the early morning was the best time; as he said,

The Sovereign Lord has given me an instructed tongue,
   to know the word that sustains the weary.
He wakens me morning by morning,
   wakens my ear to listen like one being taught.

(Isaiah 50:4; my emphasis)

Isaiah learned to shorten his sleep, to be disciplined in the use of his early morning time and actually to allow the Lord to waken him each morning so that the first moments of the day were filled with the presence of the Lord before the intrusion of anything from the world or even from those nearest and dearest to him. It makes a tremendous difference to the day if we can discipline ourselves to allow the Spirit of God to wake us morning by morning so that His Spirit permeates our spirit from the first conscious moments of the day.

KNOWING THE TRUTH

"You will know the truth," Jesus promised, "and the truth will set you free" (John 8:32). But how will we know the truth? Jesus prefaced His promise with the condition:

> If you hold to my teaching, you are really my disciples. Then you will know the truth . . .
>
> (John 8:31–32)

The Lord does not wish any of His disciples to be confused. He wants us to know the truth. He is longing to communicate His Word clearly to us. It is the work of the enemy to deceive the people of God, for he is the father of lies. But God has already made provision for the battle that each of us has to wage to hold fast to the truth. He has provided for us the clear teaching of the Lord Jesus and He has carefully collected and preserved His Word over many centuries. The revelation of God's truth that began with the patriarchs of ancient Israel and concluded with the vision of John on the island of Patmos contains all that is necessary to enable us to understand the nature and purposes of God; to teach us His Word and His ways and to lead us into mature discipleship.

There is no reason why any believer of ordinary intelligence should be deceived, because God has provided us with both His Word and His Spirit. It is the Spirit that brings the Word to life and enlightens our understanding. It is this combination of the

Word of God and the Spirit of God that we need for testing what we receive when we stand in the council of the Lord. None of us is infallible, and however experienced we are at seeking the face of God and listening quietly to Him we should always weigh carefully whatever we believe we are receiving to make sure it is indeed *divine* revelation – a word from the Lord and not the product of our own imagination.

As a rule of thumb there are three simple tests which should always be applied. They form three basic questions which we should always ask:

1. Does what I am receiving conform to the nature and purposes of God and my knowledge and experience of Him?
2. Does it conform to Scripture?
3. Does it witness to the Spirit within me?

The first two questions do require a sound knowledge of Scripture. In fact there is no substitute for familiarity with the Bible – the whole Bible, not just parts of it, because God has chosen to reveal Himself progressively over a very long period. This revelation was completed in the Lord Jesus Christ. Consequently the teaching of the New Testament is needed in order to understand the incomplete picture of God given through the Old Testament. To deny such a statement would be to say that the person and work of the Lord Jesus Christ were unnecessary.

If we are to seek the face of God and learn to listen to Him we must know Him, which means knowing the ways of God, knowing Him so well that you cannot mistake His response when you spread some important matter before Him in intercession. Always remember that God is love. God is faithful. He is forgiving, merciful, and just in all His ways. Moreover, God is unchanging; as He was in the beginning so He is today and ever will be. He is absolutely reliable, and can be relied upon absolutely.

The third test given above may be subjective and therein lies considerable danger for the unwary. But if the person seeking the face of God is a mature believer, well grounded in the Scriptures and used to moving in the Holy Spirit, the danger is minimised, for such a believer will always exercise caution, test carefully what is being received and seek confirmation in other ways if divine revelation is sought on some weighty matter.

The witness of the Holy Spirit within us can become an objective test when combined with the other two essentially Biblically based checks. Leaders, in particular, often have to give an instant judgment when they are leading a meeting in which a prophetic word is given. It is for this reason that leaders need to be men and women of great maturity so that however experienced they are in listening to the Holy Spirit within them, their personal knowledge of God and their knowledge of the Bible, drawn from years of experience, acts both as a check and as a balance upon the more subjective witness of the Spirit within them.

For the individual believer seeking in their quiet times to listen to God, there is no quick and easy route. There is no substitute for the study of Scripture. Merely reading books about the Bible will not do; we need to know the Word itself. But we also need to know Jesus; to know Him so well from the Gospels that, like the sheep who recognise the voice of their own shepherd, in Jesus' own teaching (John 10), we easily recognise the voice of the Lord.

As we come to know the Father, through the Son, the Holy Spirit is able to work more effectively within us. Then, as we seek the face of God, we learn to listen attentively, receptively, submissively, and above all expectantly.

God, who is faithful, will always respond when we approach Him with the childlike simplicity of the boy Samuel:

> Speak, LORD, for your servant is listening.
>
> (1 Samuel 3:9)

QUESTIONS

1. 2 Chronicles 7:14. How do we seek the face of God?
2. Isaiah 6:9 (see also Matthew 13:15; Luke 8:10):

> Be ever hearing, but never understanding:
>   be ever seeing, but never perceiving.

What does this mean?

3. Jeremiah 32:1–25. Jeremiah did not know why he had to buy the field. How important is it for the prophet, as a messenger of God, to understand the message?
4. Hosea 13:6:

> When I fed them, they were satisfied . . .
>   then they forgot me.

What can we (the Church) learn from the 'cycle' of Israel's history?

CHAPTER 7

LISTENING WITH DISCERNMENT

Discernment is hugely important for twenty-first-century Christians. We live in an age of deception when Biblical values are being challenged at every point of public life. Modern secular humanist values and concepts date back to the beginnings of the Age of Enlightenment, but have been promoted with ever-increasing strength since the end of the Second World War which left a huge moral vacuum and a legacy of spiritual scepticism.

DISCERNING DECEPTION
The development of the Internet has vastly increased the opportunities for fraud and deception. Identity theft and increasingly sophisticated scams have affected millions since the introduction of online banking facilities. But the most insidious forms of moral corruption have come through the massive output of pornography, freely available on Internet sites, which can be downloaded by children and seen on their mobile phones.

This kind of corruption was foreseen by Paul when writing to the Christian community in Rome, where city life was already reflecting the depths of depravity to which humanity can sink. Paul said,

> The wrath of God is being revealed from heaven against all the godlessness and wickedness of men who suppress the truth by their wickedness.
>
> (Romans 1:18)

Paul saw that once truth is suppressed, there is no limit to the corruption that will spread throughout society. He outlined the stages in this process of social degeneration which he saw as beginning with a denial of the God of Creation, although "his eternal power and divine nature . . . have been clearly seen, being understood from what has been made, so that men are without excuse" (Romans 1:20). In the final stage, God gives people over "to a depraved mind, to do what ought not to be done" (Romans 1:28). They become "filled with every kind of wickedness, evil, greed and depravity. They are full of envy, murder, strife, deceit and malice" (1:29).

Paul's warnings went unheeded, and the glorification of sexual perversion and violence in public entertainment, from which so many Christians suffered cruel martyrdom, became a major factor in the corruption of society that eventually led to the downfall of the Roman Empire. The excesses in the Roman amphitheatres were a sophisticated development of practices that had been common in cities as far back as the time of Sodom and Gomorrah. There is a significant hint of this in Genesis 15:16 where it is recorded that "the sin of the Amorites [had] not yet reached its full measure". The Amorites were noted for their homosexual practices and bestiality. Abraham was told that he personally would not be allowed to settle in the land but that his descendants would return. The implication is that the Israelites would be an instrument of divine judgment upon the Amorites.

According to Ezekiel 16:49–50 the sins of Sodom and Gomorrah were not only that they did "detestable things" before the Lord, but that they were "arrogant, overfed and unconcerned; they did not help the poor and needy". In the teaching of Jesus these "hidden" sins are roundly condemned, as demonstrated in His charges of hypocrisy against the Pharisees, who were outwardly righteous but "inside they [were] full of greed and self-indulgence" (Matthew 23:25). According to Matthew these warnings came right at the end of Jesus' earthly ministry, shortly before He talked to His disciples about signs of the end of the age, a discourse which began with warnings about deception:

> Watch out that no-one deceives you. For many will come in my name, claiming, "I am the Christ," and will deceive many.
>
> (Matthew 24:4–5)

Jesus repeated the warning about false prophets who would appear and deceive many people (Matthew 24:11) and ended with a further warning about false Christs and false prophets performing "signs and miracles" capable of deceiving even the elect (Matthew 24:24).

The ability to discern deception is clearly of great importance in the teaching of Jesus. It is therefore essential for Christians to be able to practise "discernment" which enables believers to know the difference between right and wrong and between true and false. It was the inability to do this among the spiritual leaders of Israel that led to the exile in Babylon, according to the prophet Ezekiel. He reported receiving a word from the Lord:

Her priests do violence to my law and profane my holy things; they do not distinguish between the holy and the common; they teach there is no difference between the unclean and the clean . . .

(Ezekiel 22:26)

He said that her prophets whitewashed the deeds of the people by giving "false visions and lying divinations", even giving words, supposedly from God, that the Lord had not spoken (Ezekiel 22:28).

HOLINESS AND SEPARATION

Throughout the Bible the covenant people of God are urged to be separated from the world. Abraham started life as a pagan, being brought up in the household of his father Terah, who was a worshipper of other gods (Joshua 24:2). God said to him,

Leave your country, your people and your father's household and go to the land I will show you.

I will make you into a great nation
    and I will bless you . . .
and all peoples on earth
    will be blessed through you.

(Genesis 12:1–3)

Abraham's separation from his polytheistic family prepared the way for God to establish a covenant with him and his descendants, which would distinguish them from all other nations. The importance of this distinction was seen by Moses when pleading for the presence of the Lord to go with him:

If your Presence does not go with us, do not send us up from here. How will anyone know that you are pleased with me and with your people unless you go with us? What else will distinguish me and your people from all the other people on the face of the earth?

(Exodus 33:15–16)

It was this covenant relationship with God that distinguished the people of Israel from all the other people in the world and it was His presence among them that was the distinguishing mark. But God was a holy God, utterly different from the physical creation which was the work of His own hands. He could not be represented by wood and stone, as were the gods of the other nations. Therefore, the people of Israel had to be different. Hence the strong warning given to Moses at the beginning of the Ten Commandments:

I am the LORD your God, who brought you out of Egypt, out of the land of slavery.

You shall have no other gods before me.

You shall not make for yourself an idol in the form of anything in heaven above or on the earth beneath or in the waters below. You shall not bow down to them or worship them; for I, the LORD your God, am a jealous God, punishing the children for the sin of the fathers to the third and fourth generation of those who hate me, but showing love to a thousand generations of those who love me and keep my commandments.

(Exodus 20:1–6)

Christians believe that the covenant relationship which God established with Israel from the time of Abraham has been extended to the Gentiles; to those whose lives have been redeemed through the blood of the Lord Jesus. This, of course, does not mean that the sons of Abraham by birth have been replaced by Gentiles. Paul makes this abundantly clear in Romans 11:1 where he asks the question, "Did God reject his people?" He answers this with an emphatic "By no means!" And in Ephesians 1:5 he says that God "predestined us to be adopted as his sons through Jesus Christ, in accordance with his pleasure and will". Paul was well aware of the spiritual significance of this statement for Gentiles, because under Greek law an adopted son could not be disinherited. The child had been "chosen" and therefore would be automatically included in the will of his father for an inheritance. Thus his position in the family was even more secure than that of a birth child.

Those who are redeemed in Christ come under the same requirements of holiness as the children of the promise who are children of Abraham by birth. To both Jew and Gentile believer God says,

> Give ear and come to me;
>> hear me, that your soul may live.
> I will make an everlasting covenant with you,
>> my faithful love promised to David.

(Isaiah 55:3)

This promise of God's love is followed by a reminder of the holy separation of God.

> "For my thoughts are not your thoughts,
>> neither are your ways my ways," declares the LORD.
> "As the heavens are higher than the earth,
>> so are my ways higher than your ways
>> and my thoughts than your thoughts."

(Isaiah 55:8–9)

This is an important statement for all those who wish to hear from the Lord. We cannot hear from God, who is utterly holy, if our minds are filled with unclean thoughts. We cannot hear from God if we are preoccupied with relationship problems that fill our minds with deep resentment or vengeful thoughts towards others. We cannot hear from God if our attention is dominated by worldly ambition and drives to succeed in business or politics, or by social status objectives. We cannot hear from God if our ears have iPods clamped to them, polluting our brains with the lyrics of pop songs that fill our minds with ungodly thoughts and lustful desires. All these things are a barrier to the Holy Spirit. As Jesus said, "No-one can serve two masters" (Matthew 6:24). The teaching of the Bible is quite uncompromising, that we cannot hear from God unless we are prepared to relegate the things of this world to a meaningless status in our code of values and we are prepared to have times when we shut out material things completely, so that we can have times of quietness, of reflection upon the Word of God, and of being open to the Holy Spirit.

FALSE PROPHETS

The history of both Israel and the early Church shows the troubles caused by false prophets. Jeremiah, in particular, suffered from them. The false prophets often brought messages to people which were popular and gained significant support for their authors, often to the detriment of the true prophet. One of the most blatant examples recorded in the Bible is the incident were King Jehoshaphat was contemplating joining forces with King Ahab to attack the Syrian city of Ramoth Gilead.

Dressed in their royal robes, the king of Israel and Jehoshaphat king of Judah were sitting on their thrones at the threshing-floor by the entrance to the gate of Samaria, with all the prophets prophesying before them.

(2 Chronicles 18:9)

This must have been an amazing sight, with 400 prophets prancing and dancing and shouting around the two kings in the presence of a large crowd. It would have been an intimidating experience for the lone prophet Micaiah to give a contrary prophecy in the face of the unanimous testimony of the 400. He was rewarded with scorn, abuse, physical attack and imprisonment; but he nevertheless gave the message he believed he had heard from God, the truth of which was soon to be confirmed by a disastrous defeat at the hands of the enemy.

The false prophets often lived in community and engaged in ecstatic utterances with inappropriate behaviour in contrast to the lone men of God who often risked their lives to bring the true Word of the Lord into difficult situations with unpopular messages. The false prophets often used to encourage one another by repeating prophecies and adding to them. Jeremiah complained about all the religious leaders of his day:

> From the least to the greatest,
>   all are greedy for gain;
> prophets and priests alike,
>   all practise deceit.
> They dress the wound of my people
>   as though it were not serious.
> "Peace, peace," they say,
>   when there is no peace.

(Jeremiah 8:10b –11)

Jeremiah gives us an insight into his own means of hearing from God. He speaks about standing in the council of the Lord, which no doubt is a reflection of his own quiet times of solitude when he was seeking to hear from God in response to the situation he saw around him in Jerusalem or on the international front. In the face of a growing threat of invasion from the immensely cruel Babylonian army, he pleaded with the people:

> Do not listen to what the prophets are prophesying to you;
>> they fill you with false hopes.
> They speak visions from their own minds,
>> not from the mouth of the LORD.

> (Jeremiah 23:16)

To reinforce the urgency and authenticity of his own warnings he asked,

> Which of them has stood in the council of the LORD
>> to see or to hear his word?
>> Who has listened and heard his word?
> See, the storm of the LORD
>> will burst out in wrath . . .

> (Jeremiah 23:18–19)

He quoted God as saying,

> I did not send these prophets,
>> yet they have run with their message;
> I did not speak to them,
>> yet they have prophesied.

> (Jeremiah 23:21)

He then brought the most serious accusation he could utter, as a word from God:

> If they had stood in my council,
>> they would have proclaimed my words to my people
>> and would have turned them from their evil ways . . .

(Jeremiah 23:22)

This word reflects the heart of God who did not want to see judgment and suffering brought upon his covenant people. As Isaiah records,

> Yet the LORD longs to be gracious to you;
>> he rises to show you compassion.
> For the LORD is a God of justice . . .

(Isaiah 30:18)

How different the history of Israel not only could but *would* have been, if only the people had listened to the true prophets sent by God! This is clearly stated in Isaiah 48:17–18:

> This is what the LORD says –
>> your Redeemer, the Holy One of Israel:
> "I am the LORD your God,
>> who teaches you what is best for you,
>> who directs you in the way you should go.
> If only you had paid attention to my commands,
>> your peace would have been like a river . . ."

A similar message is given in Psalm 81:13–14:

If my people would but listen to me,
    if Israel would follow my ways,
how quickly would I subdue their enemies . . .

This is probably a reflection of the promise given to Solomon at the dedication of the temple in the well-known words of 2 Chronicles 7:14:

If my people, who are called by my name, will humble themselves and pray and seek my face and turn from their wicked ways, then will I hear from heaven and will forgive their sin and will heal their land.

WHAT IS DISCERNMENT?

Discernment is *not* one of the spiritual gifts listed by Paul in 1 Corinthians 12. This is for the very simple reason that discernment is open to all believers in the Lord Jesus and is not limited to those who receive gifts of the Holy Spirit. It is not dependent upon receiving a particular spiritual gift which (apart from tongues) is given as a means for carrying out a task, usually associated with a ministry.

In a brilliant passage in 1 Corinthians 2, argued with typical Pauline logic, the apostle expands upon Jeremiah's exhortation:

"Let not the wise man boast of his wisdom
    or the strong man boast of his strength
    or the rich man boast of his riches,
but let him who boasts boast about this:
    that he understands and knows me,
that I am the LORD, who exercises kindness,
    justice and righteousness on earth,

for in these I delight,"
declares the LORD.

(Jeremiah 9:23–24)

Paul uses this to say that just as no one knows the thoughts of a man except that man himself, in the same way no-one knows the thoughts of God except the Spirit of God. We have received the Spirit of God so that we may understand the things of God. Human beings who don't have the Holy Spirit cannot understand spiritual things because they can be spiritually discerned only through the mind of Christ.

This is a fulfilment of the promise of Jesus to send the Counsellor, the Holy Spirit, from the Father, who would teach His disciples all things. In the same context Jesus called His disciples "friends" because everything He had learned from His Father, He had made known to them. He then promised,

I have much more to say to you, more than you can now bear. But when he, the Spirit of truth, comes, he will guide you into all truth. He will not speak on his own; he will speak only what he hears, and he will tell you what is yet to come.

(John 16:12–13)

This promise was fulfilled at Pentecost as the disciples waited in Jerusalem in obedience to the Lord's last command before His ascension. The coming of the Holy Spirit transformed the disciples, giving them the power to witness in the city that had so recently crucified their Master and preparing the way of the gospel to go out to the ends of the earth. Paul recognised the significance of the ministry gifts that were given in the church, "so that the body of Christ may be built up until we all reach unity in the faith and in the knowledge of the Son of God and become mature, attaining to the whole measure of the fullness of Christ" (Ephesians 4:12–13). But what was this maturity in the faith of which Paul spoke? We have to turn to Hebrews to see a clear answer.

In Hebrews 5:11 the believers are said to be "slow to learn". We don't know which group of Christians is being addressed here, but they had evidently had the gospel in their community for some time because it is said that they themselves ought to be teachers of others. Instead, they still needed someone to teach them "the elementary truths of God's word all over again" (Hebrews 5:12). They were in need of milk like infants instead of solid food as mature adults. This is followed by the important statement,

> But solid food is for the mature, who by constant use have trained themselves to distinguish good from evil.
>
> (Hebrews 5:14)

What is meant here is that those who are familiar with the Word of God, constantly reading and studying it, become so familiar with the truth that they are immediately able to discern the presence of false prophecy or false teaching. This is similar to a bank clerk who becomes so familiar with genuine banknotes, handling them every day, that he or she is quickly able to discern a counterfeit note. Knowing the truth sets us free from falsehood and guards us against those who bring counterfeit teaching, trying to deceive even the faithful. There will, in every Christian community, be some who lack maturity, especially those who are new in the faith. They need to be guarded by those who are mature believers, who know the Word of God so well that they are able to perceive the attacks of the enemy as he tries to deceive unwary believers.

It is not only the task of pastors, professional ministers and preachers to guard the flock. It is the task of all mature Christians who know their Bibles, who are familiar with the whole Word of God, not just the nice little bits that are often found in Bible-reading notes, but the difficult passages as well. Paul's testimony to the Ephesian elders, who came to Miletus when he was on his final journey back to Jerusalem, was that he had not hesitated to preach "anything that would be helpful" to them (Acts 20:20). Paul meant that he had not simply preached the good news about salvation in Jesus but that he had preached the *whole Word of God*, bringing people to the conviction of sin before bringing them to faith in Christ. This is something that is so often lacking in Christian preaching today. Jesus said that when the Holy Spirit came he would "convict the world of guilt in regard to sin and righteousness and judgment" (John 16:8).

Paul had clearly understood the whole Word of God and he was able to testify,

> I have not hesitated to proclaim to you the whole will of God. Keep watch over yourselves and all the flock of which the Holy Spirit has made you overseers. Be shepherds of the church of God, which he bought with his own blood.
>
> (Acts 20:27–28)

Peter declares that we are all part of a "chosen people, a royal priesthood, a holy nation, a people belonging to God" (1 Peter 2:9). Therefore, we all share in the task of teaching the whole Word of God to others and guarding the flock against deception by constantly proclaiming the truth, so that deception finds no weak point of entry to bring corruption into the Body of Christ. This is the shared task of all mature believers – to learn to listen to the

Lord and to exercise discernment under the direction of the Spirit of God.

QUESTIONS

1. Why did Jesus give a number of warnings about deception?
2. Can Christians be distinguished from other people in today's society?
3. If the people of Israel had listened to their prophets their history would have been different. Is this relevant today?
4. Read Hebrews 5:11 – 6:3 and discuss.

About Issachar
Ministries

Paradigm Shift

The past 20 years has witnessed a major change in the whole social and cultural life of Britain which has produced a paradigm shift in the spiritual climate of the nation. Britain is no longer a Christian nation and there is no acknowledgement of God by our political rulers or in the media.

The Judaeo-Christian heritage of the Britain is rapidly being dissipated, undermining the foundations of the nation. Secular humanism is rampant and Islam is crouching at the door ready to exploit the spiritual vacuum as Christianity retreats and surrenders the land.

But the Lord still has a faithful remnant in churches throughout the land as well as many believers who are isolated and lonely. The Holy Spirit is already at work linking believers together in home-based groups where they study the word of God and pray together.

THE BATTLE IS THE LORD'S

2 Chronicles 20 gives an inspiring example of what God can do with a nation where the people fully put their trust in him. When the people admitted "We do not know what to do, but our eyes are upon you." God's response was "Do not be afraid or discouraged ... for the battle is not yours, but God's." Then came the command, "Stand firm and see the deliverance of the Lord." But the people could not have responded to this command if they had not already been prepared through the word of God. This had been accomplished through two missions undertaken by Jehoshaphat. The first is recorded in 2 Chronicles 17.7 when Jehoshaphat "sent his officials to teach in the towns of Judah." The second mission followed a time of backsliding when Jehoshaphat had foolishly entered into an alliance with King Ahab. Jehoshaphat repented and undertook a second mission which he personally led throughout the land "and turned them back to the Lord, the God of their fathers." (2 Chronicles 19.4)

AN ISSACHAR PEOPLE

Most people in Britain today do not know God and have no knowledge of the Bible. It is God's purpose to mobilise the faithful remnant of believers and equip them for the task of taking his word to the people. God is looking for a people like the tribe of Issachar who "understood the times' and knew what should be done" (I Chronicles 12.32). It is for this reason that C and M Ministries trust changed its name to Issachar Ministries to help provide resources for the people of God so that they could face the task of transforming the nation.

STRATEGY

Issachar Ministries believe that the time has come to undertake a mission to equip believers as Jehoshaphat taught people the word of God in his time. There is a team available to visit churches in Britain to share vision, provide resources, and build up a network of Christians who are seeking to transform their community.

Issachar Ministries is working with other Christian leaders to create links between local Christian groups and to provide the means whereby their voice can be heard by national Church leaders and by Christians in Parliament.

This study booklet is just one of a wider and growing number of resources available to Christians for this task.

FOR MORE INFORMATION CONTACT:

Issachar Ministries

Moggerhanger Park, Bedford, MK44 3RW
Registered Charity Number: 1029797

Telephone: 01767 641006 – extension 211
Fax: 01767 641515
Office E-Mail: jackie@issacharministries.co.uk
Website: www.issacharministries.co.uk

About the Author

The Rev Dr Clifford Hill MA BD PhD is a sociologist and theologian. His pastoral ministry has been in inner-city areas of London including a long ministry in the East End during which he also held a Senior Lectureship in the Sociology of Religion in London University. He was the founder of the Newham Community Renewal Programme, one of the largest urban mission organisations in Britain. He also founded Prophetic Word Ministries which had an extensive international ministry from 1982 to 2005 with its flagship magazine, Prophecy Today.

C & M Ministries Trust was officially formed as an independent charity in 1993, although it had been operating as a ministry under the umbrella of Prophetic Word Ministries (PWM) Trust since the early 1980s. The Issachar Trust is an arm of C & M Ministries Trust.

Clifford is the author of more than 40 books, covering a range of subjects including race and community relations, socio-political studies, biblical commentaries and research studies on the family, as well as many journal papers, tapes, CDs and other resources, including some written jointly with his wife Monica.

We hope you enjoyed reading this
Sovereign World book.
For more details of other Sovereign
books and new releases see our website:

www.sovereignworld.com

Find us on Twitter @sovereignworld

Our authors welcome your feedback on their books.
Please send your comments to our offices.
You can request to subscribe to
our email and mailing list online or by writing to:

**Sovereign World Ltd, PO Box 784,
Ellel, Lancaster, LA1 9DA, United Kingdom
info@sovereignworld.com**

Sovereign World titles are available from
all good Christian bookshops and eBook vendors.

For information about our distributors in the UK,
USA, Canada, South Africa, Australia and Singapore, visit:
www.sovereignworld.com/trade

If you would like to help us send a copy of this book and
many other titles to needy pastors in developing countries,
please write for further information or send your gift to:

Sovereign World Trust, PO Box 777,
Tonbridge, Kent TN11 0ZS
United Kingdom
www.sovereignworldtrust.org.uk
The Sovereign World Trust is a registered charity